WINNING WITHOUT LOSING

66 strategies for succeeding in business while living a happy and balanced life

by Martin Bjergegaard and Jordan Milne

PROFILE BOOKS

First published in Great Britain in 2013 by
Profile Books Ltd
3a Exmouth House
Pine Street
Exmouth Market
London EC1R 0JH
www.profilebooks.com

10 9 8 7 6 5 4 3 2 1

A CIP catalogue record for this book is available from the British Library.

ISBN: 978 1 78125 150 8
eISBN: 978 1 78283 006 1

Typeset in Book Antiqua by MacGuru Ltd
info@macguru.org.uk

Printed and bound in Britain by Bell and Bain Ltd

Photo credits
Getty Images: Steve Bronstein, p. 130; Chris Craymer, p. 266; D-BASE, p. 78;
Dwight Eschliman, p. 214; Ed Freeman, p. 68; Frank Herholdt, p. 82; Charlotte
Hu, p. 140; Harry Kikstra, p. 254; John Lund, p. 250; Gregor Schuster, p. 74;
Henrik Sorensen, p. 20; Freudenthal Verhagen, p. 40.
Daniel Karlsson, p. 289 (photo of Christian Stadil).
Shutterstock: leedsn, p. 150; Charles B. Ming Onn, p. 98; Vitalii Nesterchuk, p. 210;
Gergo Orban, p. 172; trappy76, p. 196.
Thinkstock: Altrendo Images, p. 144; Michael Blann, pp. 30, 104, 136; Mike Powell,
p. 114.

DEDICATION

To my friends and partners at Rainmaking who make our shared adventure so much fun every day. To my wife Annika for consistently believing in me, even when I seriously doubted if I had what it took to get a decent book to market. And to my daughter, Mynte, for giving me a terrific reason to passionately search for the recipe for a balanced and whole life.

– Martin

For being lucky enough to have family and friends who want me to be happy. For being fortunate enough to have the opportunity to choose the direction of my own life. And to Martin for making the experience of writing this book a true example of what we are writing about.

– Jordan

THE MYTHS OF HARD WORK AND SACRIFICE

Things used to be simple. We could rely on some basic truths:

- The harder you work, the more money you make
- Success comes with sacrifice
- It is hard to be successful
- You need to choose between being a family person or a business person
- Balance is for retirement or after the 'big exit'
- There is no time to do it all
- Pushing yourself is necessary
- The winner is the one who works the hardest
- The more hours you work, the more impact you will have
- Being an entrepreneur means no holiday for several years
- Family and friends are for Sundays

Today these statements are no longer true. We face a new reality. Welcome to the age of Winning without Losing.

THANK YOU!

The words on these pages and their message would not have been possible without the help and inspiration of many great people. Thank you – we are grateful. There are too many to name (please forgive us) but we will try:

Test readers, our most active online contributors, and others who have truly helped and supported us: Sergey Turko, Fred Pullin, Søren Houen, Annie Milne, Brian Milne, Isla Milne, Avaleigh Milne, Monica Pereira, John Terry, Anders Bjergegaard, Matias Møl Dalsgaard, Artas Bartas, Sapumal Jayaratne, J. Winslow, Antonio José Arderius Baca-Balboa, Karen Cordingley, Kræn Hansen, Marni Galison, Prasad Chougule, Peter Tatishev, Jannick B. Pedersen, Roxanne Varza, Gregg Vanourek, Henning Daverne, Ole Høyer, Stever Robbins, Robert Gass, Prashant Raizada, Peer Kølendorf, Clint Nelsen, Jesper H. Andersen, Rasmus Ankersen, Prakash Idnani, Michael Bodekær, Søren Hougaard, Jesper Klit, Nicolai Frisch, Martin Markussen, Eileen Sutton, Jakob Algreen-Ussing, Linda Hickman, Jesper Krogh Jørgensen, Mike Michalowicz, Annika Dehlén Bjergegaard, Allan Rønne, Valdemar Rønne Jensen, Kim Johnson – and Martin's 5-year-old daughter Mynte who helped pick the original cover design.

Our 25 role models: Chad Troutwine, Markus Moberg, Torsten Hvidt, Henrik Lind, Randi Komisar, Nick Mikhailovsky, Caterina Fake, Peter Mægbæk, Christian Stadil, David Cohen, Derek Sivers, Ben Way, Bill Liao, Tony Hsieh, Jake Nickell, Maxim Spiridonov,

Martin Thorborg, John Vechey, Jason Fried, Claus Meyer, Sophie Vandebroek, Brad Feld, Mitch Thrower, N. R. Murthy, Xiangdong Zhang.

The Winning without Losing team: Bent Haugland (project management), Lélia Peuchamiel and Nele Wollert (online community), Thomas Michaelsen Pethick and Johan Bichel Lindegaard (web development), Thomas Holm-Hansen, Jonathan Friedman, Kalimaya Krabbe, Linda Ghabain, Raminta Gobiene, Zivile Bagdonaite (assistants), Martin Skjerbæk, Natasha Larsen and Anine Hagemann (translation), Nana Christiansen (text), Ela Rudzinska (bookkeeping), Jesper Klingenberg (website), Patricia Hepe (book design) and Mari-Anne Daura (marketing).

The Rainmaking partners: Carsten Kølbek, Morten Kristensen, Morten Bjerregaard Nielsen, Mads Mathiesen, Kasper Vardrup, Alex Farcet, Kenneth Siber, Mats Stigzelius.

And last but definitely not least our editor, **Laurence Shorter**, author of the exceptionally inspiring and delightfully entertaining book *The Optimist*.

TABLE OF CONTENTS

PURPOSE THE GOOD LIFE DISCOVER RESHAPE
ENJOY SMILE FREEDOM TODAY SUCCESS DREAM
EXPONENTIAL EFFICIENCY ENERGY HAPPY
HAVE IT ALL ROLE MODELS FLOW FREEDOM
BREATHE BALANCE MOMENTUM IMPACT
SECRETS FORTUNE DOUBLE OPTIMUM
ENTHUSIASM MOVEMENT FUN PRESENCE
PEACE MOMENT POSSIBLE GROW CHANGE FOCUS
HEALTH EXCITEMENT REVOLUTION CARING

WINNING WITHOUT LOSING

FRIENDSHIP TRAVEL LOVE RELAXATION
DO WHAT YOU LOVE BE PRESENT GIVING CHOICE
FINANCIAL SUCCESS STRONG REFRESH DREAM
LEAD THE WAY A NEW MOVEMENT FOCUS
LAUGHTER JOY SPONTANEOUS SMILE
SUCCESS COURAGE DREAM EXCITEMENT

THE NEW
DUAL OPTIMUM

A LIFE OF REGRET

'I blew it.' The words came from Sam Walton, founder of Wal-Mart, and America's wealthiest man from 1982 to 1988. The utterance came on his deathbed, as he realised that he barely knew his children and grandchildren, and that his wife had, he felt, only stayed with him out of obligation. Throughout his life he had been so focused on success in business that he had reached it only to realise just how much he had sacrificed to get there. Sam had neglected the other important areas of his life – in his case, the time to build and sustain a meaningful relationship with his family. Tragically this is not an isolated case and there are numerous other accounts of people less successful than Sam who have eventually reached the same bitter conclusion.

We might assume that it is more common for those in high-profile, high-power positions with a ton of obligations and distractions to fall captive to this particular trap in life, but the reality is that what Sam experienced affects people in all positions across all industries. It affects entrepreneurs, corporate workers and government employees and is a problem from CEOs to associates alike. Families are broken, friendships starved to death and health is jeopardised, all leading to lives that will sooner or later be filled with regret. When asked to name what is most important in our lives, most people are quick to say family, friends and health. And what is one of the most commonly cited reasons for broken relationships and poor health? You guessed it: work.

In Japan so many people have died from overwork that they have given it its own term: 'Karoshi', meaning 'death from overwork'. Although Karoshi is the extreme, lesser degrees of overwork have far-reaching and cumulative effects on all elements of our lives. And after all, **most of us are not looking to simply prevent the ultimate disaster but are actively searching for the best way to live full and amazing lives**: to have success, as well as the time and energy to enjoy it.

It may seem difficult to become a successful and balanced entrepreneur or business tycoon. Every new business is a small miracle, and like a rocket going into space, it needs an enormous amount of energy to get it off the ground. It also takes an immense amount of dedication to grow your venture into something big, sustainable and widely recognised. In the face of such a profound challenge, could there really be the time and energy to accomplish this while living a happy, whole and balanced life – a life without regret?

The answer is yes. And we will show you how.

THE NEW DUAL OPTIMUM

We bring fresh news from the entrepreneurial frontier: today, possibly for the first time in history, it is actually possible to be someone who puts friends and family first, while at the same time creating a business and a fortune from scratch. We don't have to come home from work after our children are asleep and we no longer need to say no to friends suggesting a Friday beer or weekend game of football. Six to eight weeks of holiday spent travelling around the world each year, or doing something other than work to recharge you and broaden your perspectives, is not just a very real option but increasingly a prerequisite for optimum and sustainable efficiency.

As we learn more about how the human body, mind and motivation work, and as today's challenges demand a new set of skills, it becomes clear that the old strategy of simply out-working our competition is no longer the only viable way. **It is now possible to optimise our business success and personal happiness at the same time**. We call it The New Dual Optimum. With this confluence of factors at play, there no longer needs to be competition between personal and business success, and this means that one of the oldest beliefs of business life – that success requires sacrifice – is rapidly becoming outdated.

So how is personal happiness relevant to a book about business?

Having asked ourselves this very same question for a long time, we've reached the conclusion that on at least one crucial point we agree with the Dalai Lama: the purpose of life must be to get as much happiness out of it as possible. Happy people are nicer to others and better for the world than angry people. When we are happy we have more energy and are more inclined to help others. Because we all have to leave here one day, and all adhere to the same 'naked in, naked out' principle, the only logical conclusion is that we must take responsibility for having as many happy minutes, hours and days as possible in our lives.

While happiness is to a large extent determined by our genes, upbringing, choice of life partner and close relationships, work is in the top five determining factors in nearly all studies. What and whom we work with are important, as is the amount of time spent doing it. It is very hard to optimise our long-term happiness if we must work 16 hours a day, 365 days a year.

Conversely, if we were told that we were never allowed to do as much as one hour of activity that could be defined as work, then our happiness would be equally compromised.

For most of us the 'happiness optimum' lies somewhere between 30 and 60 hours of work per week. The low end of this scale typically applies if we have many other commitments, or if we are doing something we're not really engaged in. The high end of the scale applies if we have defined our project ourselves, are doing it together with people who give us energy, and don't have many other big claims on our agenda.

The great tragedy is when we push ourselves past our happiness optimum in an effort to achieve success. In the process, ironically and despite our best intentions, we also pass our efficiency optimum, and thus lose twice; we're less happy than we could have been, and we'll have less success than we could have had. Business life is full of people who, by working 10 or 20 hours less per week, could be both happier and more successful. Maybe you're one of them.

THE LAW OF DIMINISHING RETURNS

Let's look at an example. In school, many of us learned of a concept called 'diminishing returns' or 'diminishing marginal returns'. The essence is that we get a lot of value from the first unit we add, less and less from those that follow, and at a certain point each additional unit creates either zero or negative value.

We use the principle intuitively all the time, for example when we're watering flowers. The first cup of water is very useful, we don't really know if the plant needs the next one and the third results in a drowning accident. If you've ever asked others to water your plants while you were out travelling, you might have said something like 'you know, just enough, not too much'.

Formalised in the early 1800s by the British economist, politician, millionaire and author David Ricardo, the law of diminishing returns has gained status as one of the most important mathematical laws. We now know that this law also applies to other aspects of life.

Production planners have applied the law for more than 100 years. After the Second World War the advertising industry became another faithful disciple. The first 1,000 advertisements work really well, the following 1,000 have a mediocre effect, and the last 1,000 simply won't be worth it.

Athletes and their coaches know it too. When the Ethiopian long-distance runner Haile Gebrselassie set a world record in the Berlin Marathon on 30 September 2007 with a time of 2:04:26 he hadn't trained day and night in the months and years leading up to competition. Instead, what he had done was find the optimum amount of training, allowing him to beat numerous opponents who had spent far more hours on the road than him.

WHERE IS YOUR OPTIMUM EFFICIENCY?

When it comes to our working life, our education, the firm we're starting or the career we're building, most of us have at some point sensed a limit. We have tried periods of working so hard that we were ultimately no longer productive. We lost perspective, strength and motivation, and needed days or even weeks of rest to recuperate. Seth Godin, an American entrepreneur, marketing guru, blogger and bestselling author, describes how in his early days he once stayed at the office for a month straight, working constantly to meet a deadline. So far, so good, but Seth had pushed himself past the limit and was sick for the next 6 months. He had simply worked too hard and gone too far on the scale of diminishing returns. His returns were fine for a single month, but viewed over a 7-month period, he was incredibly ineffective. So where do you think your optimum is? If you only think about optimising your efforts at work, how many hours a week should you spend at the office? 30? 70? 100?

We might think it depends on what type of work we're doing. And we're absolutely right. If our tasks are routine, do not require any heavy thinking, and don't involve collaboration or creativity we can probably be productive for more hours than if we're an air traffic controller or a heart surgeon. The less concentration and focus an activity requires, the more hours we can keep doing it. We don't want air traffic controllers who sit in front of the screen for 100 hours a week.

Some work too little relative to their optimum efficiency, others too much.

As entrepreneurs and leaders we are passionate about our projects. We have dreams and dare to pursue them. Add to this our attitude towards work and you get some extremely driven people. Our task is, however, anything but routine. **We are more comparable to the air traffic controller, who at every moment must be aware, make critical choices and cooperate with others to ensure success.**

Many of us still believe, however, that we achieve more if we work 70 hours a week than if we work 50. This logic works well in many industrial settings, where a machine can weld 10 units per hour or pack 5 pallets with tea bags in 30 minutes. However, a new kind of logic is needed when we are considering the kinds of tasks that entrepreneurs are faced with.

Of course, it isn't as simple as swapping some time at the desk for some time on the couch. Actually, the interesting thing isn't the relationship between 'work' and 'non-work'. Someone should invent a better word than work, because the new generation of entrepreneurs and executives don't 'work'. We play, do what we love and unfold our talents and dreams.

We have more in common with athletes, musicians and sculptors than with the traditional factory or office worker. But even artists and athletes experience diminishing – and ultimately negative – marginal returns. Nobody knows better than painters and writers that inspiration is necessary to create a masterpiece. Inspiration can't be found by sitting in front of the canvas or desk 100 hours a week. It takes much more. Balance is an important piece of that puzzle.

BALANCE IS NOT FOR SISSIES

We talk a lot about balance in this book. What we mean by the word 'balance' is 'what you consider to be a good life'. We don't profess to know your bucket list or the ideal way for you to distribute your waking hours. What we are doing is urging you to think about it, make a conscious choice, and dare to design your own life in the way that is optimal for you.

Perhaps you are now thinking something along the lines of: 'Balance sounds boring, weak, and uninteresting. I don't want balance; I want an exciting life, with sensational projects, lots of success and a wild day of kite surfing.'

Maybe you're right and maybe you should give this book to your sensitive cousin. But just play along with us for two more minutes. Why? Because balance might just be the key to you living that ideal life.

For most people, an ideal life is some combination of the following:

- Having positive relationships with other people
- Being good at something
- Having financial freedom
- Feeling good physically and mentally
- Being on top of things and in control of your life
- Contributing positively to some greater purpose

To bring all of these elements together, and to have each one play an important role in our life, takes quite a bit of effort. It requires thought and intelligent strategies. It requires balance.

No matter how much we love our work, leaving room for little else won't be a route to sustainable happiness. We also need to give and receive love, to get completely different inputs and experiences, to use our body and to have fun with old and new friends.

On the other hand, it may be that if we only spend 10 hours a week working on our project because we are too busy partying, watching TV and spending someone else's money, we actually regret never reaching the goals we set for ourselves. The point is that **whether we like it or not, there is balance or imbalance in our life and we are the only one who can identify it and do something about it**. Balance is not for sissies; it is for the courageous. And it is definitely possible.

THE MACHO AND THE MARTYR HAVE BOTH GONE OUT OF FASHION

So if balance is for the courageous, then is being 'macho' and boasting that we have slept only 2 hours a night for a week because we were busy working on an important project no longer impressive? You bet it is. As most of us have learned more about how our body and brain function, we are becoming aware that living the macho life is more foolish than impressive. At the end of the day we will have lost more efficiency than we have gained by skipping sleep, leisure time and exercise.

Don't get us wrong; pushing ourselves to peak performance is of course still worth striving for. For example, to beat our personal speed record on a 10K run, to learn a new skill (even if it is difficult), or to devise and execute a perfect sales pitch, is admirable. **But to push ourselves and actively reduce our overall effectiveness, resulting in feeling bad – well, that's just plain stupid**.

Some of us have a greater tendency to play the martyr card than the macho card. We work 16 hours straight to allow ourselves some self-pity. If we can moan and complain a little so that others will also start to feel sorry for us, the strange pleasure becomes even greater. But honestly, how great is that? We probably have some old aunt who can serve us the raw, unlimited version of this kind of behaviour. Is that really where we want to be headed?

It's always harder to see it in ourselves, but try to think about whether you know anyone who, a little too often, plays either the macho or martyr card. Perhaps a friend or colleague who either likes to brag about his efforts, or pities herself for her sacrifices. And you can probably see through them before their first sentence is even finished, right? But remember, you are just as transparent.

SEARCHING THE GLOBE

This project was conceived on a midwinter's day in 2009, when the two of us (Martin and Jordan) met for the first time in Copenhagen. We discovered that in addition to being entrepreneurs, we shared a passion for the conscious pursuit of a new paradigm for ambitious entrepreneurs and executives. A way to be successful without having to accept sacrifices in your personal life.

Together we have spent the past two years exploring the globe, speaking to hundreds of entrepreneurs in search of examples who ticked that special box, who were both extremely successful and happy and balanced: outliers who challenged our thinking about the correlation between success and sacrifice. As we searched, we soon discovered that there was indeed something of a movement under way, **a genuine shift towards more sustainable and humane approaches to work**.

These entrepreneurs were generous enough to reveal to us what they had done to achieve what so many thought to be impossible. We were humbled by the experience.

Most of them created their fortunes within the past decade. By approaching their work with a different attitude and new set of strategies, they have managed to be exponentially more effective than the average entrepreneur, while honouring their quality of life. In the course of building their businesses they have retained, and still enjoy, thriving relationships with family and friends, have travelled the world and relished all the great experiences life has to offer. What is even more surprising is that these entrepreneurs were not running small lifestyle businesses, but industry-changing, multimillion (even billion) dollar enterprises. They had simply found their own dual optimum.

66 PIECES OF INSPIRATION

This book is structured as 66 short essays, each of which reveals a strategy, method or insight relevant to 'winning without losing'. In them we have condensed:

1   Our personal dialogues with entrepreneurs from around the globe who have succeeded in achieving the best of both worlds;

2   Research and advice from world-renowned experts in psychology and efficiency;

3   The contributions, wisdom and inspiration of people we work, debate and live with;

and, finally:

4   Our own experiences of launching and running enterprises, including the successful company factory, Rainmaking, a 'start-up factory' which in 6 years has achieved 3 successful exits, a portfolio of eight prosperous start-ups with 50 million dollars in total revenues, and 100 employees in London, Copenhagen and Berlin. All of this while taking 6–8 weeks of holiday a year, recharging our batteries, spending time with

family and friends, travelling, playing sports, having fun and rarely working more than 45 hours per week. (In other words: yes, it is possible!)

We have divided the essays into seven sections:

#1 Efficiency Boosters: 15 strategies that will inspire you to increase your efficiency exponentially. As we will see, the relationship between input and output is by no means linear; in the world of entrepreneurship some people manage to draw an hourly income in the millions, while others fight just as hard to bring home a minimum wage as a trainee at McDonald's. Be smart and put yourself in the right category.

#2 New Ways of Doing Old Things: 5 essays that illustrate how very small adjustments to our daily routines (like thinking, learning and making to-do lists) can have a huge impact on how much we achieve – and how much fun we can have in the process.

#3 It is amazing how much time we all waste on a daily basis. Most of what we do doesn't create any real value in terms of either business performance or personal happiness. It is time to reduce the waste: 14 essays on how to **Beware the Time and Energy Wasters**.

#4 There is no reason to deny it; sometimes being an entrepreneur is tough. Our role models have had their fair share of failures too. Take a cue from their lives and get 5 empowering thoughts for **When the Road is Rough** – for a fast and not too painful comeback.

#5 Most people hope for balance, very few plan for it. Stop playing the wheel of fortune, and start applying the 10 simple elements in the section of **Balance by Design**. You will be surprised how easily balance can actually be achieved if you just factor it in from the very beginning.

#6 At the end of the day it is all about believing. We can learn dozens or even hundreds of methods and strategies to help us get to our own Dual Optimum. But if we don't, in our heart, truly believe that this place exists (at least for us) it will all just be (another) waste of time. Eleven essays about finding **A New Mindset**.

#7 When confronted with inspiration from our role models, many respond: 'Great – I am a believer – now tell me specifically what I can do right here and now.' Our book ends with a section urging you to **Take Action** with 6 essays to get you set for your own version of Winning without Losing.

NOW LET'S START.

MEET A SAMPLE OF OUR ROLE MODELS

See the rest at www.winningwithoutlosing.org
and on page 287.

MITCH THROWER:

Author, financier, co-founder of
The Active Network, Bump.com
and much more – also a
22 times Ironman triathlete.

TONY HSIEH:

CEO of Zappos.com which was
acquired by Amazon in 2009
for nearly $1 billion. Previously
founded LinkExchange and sold it
to Microsoft. Author of bestselling
book, *Delivering Happiness*.

N. R. NARAYANA MURTHY:

Indian billionaire and founder
of the global technology company Infosys. Sits on the boards
of some of the world's most
powerful companies including
HSBC, The Ford Foundation and
Unilever.

BILL LIAO:
Entrepreneur and revolutionary philanthropist. The driving force behind 7 IPOs including Xing.com.

JOHN VECHEY:
Co-founder of PopCap Games, which recently sold to EA for an estimated $1.3 billion.

CHAD TROUTWINE:
Co-founder and CEO of leading global test preparation company Veritas Prep, co-founder of Freakonomics Media, LLC and the producer of 10 feature films.

CLAUS MEYER:
Chef, entrepreneur, author and co-founder of a Nordic food empire including Noma, the #1 restaurant in the world two years running.

BRAD FELD:

Prolific investor, MD of The Foundry group and co-founder of TechStars. Recently named #1 most respected VC in the USA by *Business Insider*.

SOPHIE VANDEBROEK:

'Intrapreneur' and CTO of technology giant XEROX, with $22 billion in revenue.

JASON FRIED:

Co-founder and president of 37 Signals, co-author of *New York Times* bestseller *REWORK*.

JAKE NICKELL:

Co-founded Threadless.com with $1,000 and built it into one of the most admired e-commerce companies in America, with multimillion dollar profits.

EFFICIENCY BOOSTERS
→ 15 STRATEGIES TO INCREASE YOUR EFFICIENCY EXPONENTIALLY

When we don't meet our goals the natural response for many of us is to throw more hours at the tasks we are trying to accomplish. But that is like pushing our car uphill – instead of finding a way to get the engine started.

Sure, we can stay at the office late. But is that really what will make the difference? Adding 20% more time will at most enable us to get 20% more work done – not taking into account the fatigue we might encounter. The real question is: **what actions have the potential to make us 10, 100 or even 1,000 times more effective?**

We need a new set of strategies to guide our actions. Here are some of the most powerful and effective ones that we have learned in our quest for exponential efficiency.

#1 ASSEMBLE YOUR WHEEL

BY MARTIN BJERGEGAARD

According to Greek mythology, at the beginning of time, man and woman were stuck together like a wheel with two heads. They rolled along together with ease, unfazed by the world around them. This ease soon grew into confidence, which slowly grew into arrogance. To punish them for being arrogant the Gods sliced them down the centre, separating them forever. The myth asserts that from that day on, men and women have been lonely, tirelessly searching the world for their lost half.

Although we don't necessarily suggest reinventing the wheel or duct-taping yourself to a co-founder, there is a lesson to be learned from this myth. **If you launch your start-up alone you are the wheel sliced in half, lacking the support needed to create a thriving business**. Maybe you won't be searching the world for your lost half for eternity, but your chances of success are drastically reduced. By going it alone you are putting yourself at a huge disadvantage right out of the starting gate.

What do Adobe, Apple, Canon, Cisco, Garmin, Infosys, Intel, Microsoft, Oracle and Sun Microsystems have in common? Yes, they are all enormously successful start-ups that have gone on to become international icons, but there is more. Each one was founded by at least two entrepreneurs.

How far would Bill Gates have come without Paul Allen? Would N. R. Narayana Murthy have been able to create Infosys all by himself? Likely not. But when Murthy got together with his six co-founders they created one of India's largest tech companies, making all seven of them billionaires in the process and landing him on the boards of some of the world's most powerful institutions including HSBC, Unilever, UN Foundation, INSEAD, Wharton and The Ford Foundation.

Maybe you are one of the thousands of hopefuls across the globe looking to take your idea to the next level by snagging a much-coveted spot at a top tier start-up accelerator? You tell yourself you're a lone wolf and that it's more courageous and admirable to attempt to build the business yourself. The evidence, however, proves otherwise. Flying solo will likely take you out of the running for joining such high-profile programmes as Techstars, Y Combinator and Startupbootcamp. Paul Graham, co-founder of Y Combinator, and David Cohen, co-founder of TechStars, have enough collective experience to know that the success rate is low for single-founder entrepreneurs. None of the top accelerators accepts single-founder teams; the odds are stacked too high against them. Looking to skip straight to venture capital funding instead? The venture capital (VC) industry generally supports this line of thinking as well and is also looking for a 'whole wheel'.

Paul Graham recently wrote an essay entitled '18 mistakes that kill start-ups'. And what, according to this legendary entrepreneur and investor, was the number one thing to steer clear of? The single founder.

EFFICIENCY BOOSTER #1:
GATHER A TEAM OF GREAT CO-FOUNDERS

#2 GET STARTED, GET MOMENTUM

BY JORDAN MILNE

In physics, momentum is equal to the product of mass times velocity. The law of conservation of linear momentum states that unless external forces are acting on a closed system of objects, the momentum of the closed system will remain constant. Unfortunately the laws of nature don't translate directly to the business world, but the general principles still apply; once an entrepreneur reaches a certain level of success, the momentum will often help them continue on that path. Getting that initial velocity can be tricky, but once you've got movement the laws of physics are on your side.

Nearly everyone has heard of Mark Zuckerberg and how he has changed the social landscape with Facebook, making billions along the way. What is perhaps less well known is that Facebook wasn't his first success (and no, it wasn't Facemash, either).

While still a student in high school an even younger Zuckerberg honed his skills by building a computer music application. Synapse, as he called it, was a music recommendation service that used artificial intelligence to learn a user's listening habits. This application would prove to be successful and he was eventually offered a buy-out from both AOL and Microsoft who also wanted to recruit the young talent. In what looks like a foreshadowing of the future, Mark turned it down. He would, however, take on this momentum to eventually build Facebook. And that early exit opportunity? A few years later he would turn down another offer, this one for $1 billion from Yahoo, while by early 2012 Facebook was estimated to be worth as much as $100 billion.

Chad Troutwine is another entrepreneur who uses the benefits of momentum to his advantage. Fresh out of university Chad set out with a partner to develop real estate in his hometown of Kansas, Missouri. Sensing an opportunity in an up-and-coming neighbourhood, Chad and his business partner began developing old warehouses into condominiums. With a few smart decisions and some learning on the fly, the two made the venture a success. The condos sold quickly, making both partners a healthy sum of money. This taste of success taught Chad many valuable lessons and gave him the confidence to tackle bigger things. The success gave Chad momentum. Armed with his previous triumph, Chad went on to co-found Veritas Prep, an international admission test training company, along with other ventures, and soon enough ended up gracing the cover of *Entrepreneur* magazine.

Even a small success can lead to credibility, contacts and the confidence to execute.

Start big if you can but don't be afraid to start small and build momentum. The business you're working on now may not be a billion dollar idea, but it could be an important step. Whatever you do, get going. Many people think they'll start when they get their 'big idea'. Get out of that mindset. Start something. It will give you momentum. Waiting will always just be waiting.

EFFICIENCY BOOSTER #2:
DON'T SIT AROUND AND WAIT.
GET OUT THERE AND START SOMETHING.

#3 GET YOUR TIMING RIGHT

BY JORDAN MILNE

From when to go in for that first kiss, to the perfect instant for making the pass to score the winning goal. People say timing is everything. This is also true in business. Just as there are benefits to riding your own energy waves, there are also benefits to riding the waves of the macro-climate.

Many entrepreneurs have met their demise partly as a result of ignoring the greater context in which they are starting their business. Numerous optimists have built fantastic products, often with cutting-edge technologies. Most consumers, however, aren't that cutting edge. Many of the other pieces of the puzzle required to enable our vision to take off may not be present. When we're looking for people to adopt our new and amazing Y, they are often still doing X, and might not be ready for the change. As always, customers will have the final say.

Alexander Bain patented the process for the fax machine in 1843, but it only started being used in 1964. Bernard Silver and Norman Woodland invented bar codes in 1948 but 20 years passed before their invention was truly utilised. Few have also heard of a company called MetaBridge. In the early 1990s MetaBridge pioneered a revolutionary technology for a 'cross media' publishing platform. Brilliant, yet it was once again 20 years too early.

What would have become a runaway success with the presence of devices such as the iPhone and Kindle turned out to be a flop due to timing. The technology was eventually acquired by other companies and MetaBridge faded away.

Caterina Fake is the co-founder of Flick'r, one of the Internet's biggest household names. Launched in 2004, Flick'r enables millions of users worldwide to organise and share their photographs and videos. Caterina is an advocate of having a good balance in your life, so we reached out to her, and in our conversation she outlined how timing played a part in the incredible success of Flick'r. Caterina explains: 'It was the perfect fit for the time and era. So much of technology is timing. When we launched in 2004 a real level of comfort in personal electronics and digital photos was coming to pass. This widespread adoption of photo-enabled devices came at a critical time that made Flick'r valuable and necessary to our users. It increased the number of digital photos exponentially, and in turn a need to store and share them.'

So how do you make sure the masses are ready for you? Part of the equation is making a conscious effort to look for movements, but don't trick yourself into thinking that you can figure it out by reading trend reports. Instead go ice fishing. **Test the water in different spots and see what the actual result is in that moment**. While you are critically testing your own concept, keep the blinders off; take advantage of the momentum of current movements.

As the famous French writer, artist and statesman Victor Hugo once said, 'There is nothing more powerful than an idea whose time has come.'

EFFICIENCY BOOSTER #3: PICK A TIMELY PROJECT

---

4 MAKE A SMALL TEST

BY MARTIN BJERGEGAARD

In 1996 McDonald's launched a series of deluxe burgers in an attempt to strengthen their position with more mature and quality-conscious customers. Three hundred million dollars was invested in the company's most ambitious product innovation to date. Focus groups, trend analysis and product development were followed by the most expensive marketing campaign the world had ever seen. Unfortunately the customers did not buy the new burgers and they were soon taken off the menu. That year, $300 million was depreciated in the head office in Illinois.

In a large company it is devastating and expensive to make such a mistake, but life goes on. Maybe an executive or two will get the boot, but the brand, the balance sheet and the organisation are most often strong enough to withstand the blow. It is very different in a start-up. Your clip only holds a limited amount of bullets and if you miss, the game is over. The cash box is empty and the trust is gone before you have even got started.

Focus groups and questionnaires are consultants' and academics' favourite tools but are lethal diversions for entrepreneurs. In a focus group, people will say what they think you or the rest of the group wants to hear. Questionnaires are ticked off without much thought about anything other than escaping from the annoyance

of the situation. **Skip the delay tactics, go straight to your potential customers and try to sell them your product**. Make a point of doing it before you have spent a fortune on finishing the product itself, otherwise you risk the customers wanting something completely different from what you have bet the farm on developing.

A leading principle in Rainmaking is that we always make a small test. This is true for a new product, a new employee, as well as a brand new company. It is always possible to design a test even though it can feel uncomfortable to be thrown into the action so early on. Many of us prefer fiddling with research and surveys as opposed to doing sales calls.

Direct contact with customers will quickly reveal if there is real potential in your idea. You can try building a demo in Wordpress, Illustrator or even papier mâché; just create something simple that gets your message across. Customers like to be involved in the development process too, so be honest and tell them you would like to have their input.

If we at Rainmaking had used the same strategy as McDonald's did with their deluxe burger we would have been shot down several times. Almost half of the start-ups we have launched in the last 5 years have been closed down, but each time with a manageable loss of time and money. By using the 'small test' method it was possible in every case to receive a real market response for a modest investment.

One such example was the launch of one of our businesses in

Oslo, Norway. We felt confident that product procurement would not be a problem so we started straight away with customer meetings. Although we did not know exactly what products we were going to sell, we had a close enough idea, which meant we could start pitching the concept to customers.

We didn't spend our time or money renting an office, because in that sector customers do not generally visit their suppliers. The only action we took was to hold dozens of meetings over a period of 4–6 months with potential buyers. In the beginning we thought things were going well because the buyers were being very responsive and friendly. This positive feeling wore off, however, when, after a second or third meeting, we asked them to commit and place an order. Almost everybody respectfully declined. What we learned was that people in Oslo are very polite. Although they had pleasantly nodded and smiled, what they really meant was 'thanks, but no thanks'. We pulled back from the project but were pleased that we hadn't spent time and money on securing the products or decorating an office because it was unlikely that we could get a foothold in the market.

Today, when we receive a request from a team of talented entrepreneurs who want us to invest time and money in them, we agree on certain tasks to accomplish and concrete goals to achieve. In that way we have something specific to work on together. This process allows us to find out if we share the same values and gives us the opportunity to see if they are good at executing these tasks. What we don't do is sit around looking at a PowerPoint deck or checking if the Excel spreadsheet is built according to the textbook. By engaging a prospective team member – or entrepreneur – in a small test, not only do you both save time and money, but the work you are doing together as part of your mutual due diligence is also much more fun and fulfilling.

EFFICIENCY BOOSTER #4:
MAKE IT A HABIT TO TEST
EVERYTHING ON A SMALL SCALE

#5 GET OUT OF THE GARAGE

BY MARTIN BJERGEGAARD

Nick Mikhailovsky smiles shyly as my Russian contact explains why he has chosen to set up a meeting between the two of us in this modern conference centre, east of central Moscow.

'Role model? I'm just an ordinary entrepreneur trying to develop my businesses and take care of my family.' Just plain ordinary is something Nick Mikhailovsky definitely is not.

Throughout his exceptional career, Nick has learned many lessons. Perhaps the greatest is that collaboration and inspiration are driving forces in entrepreneurship. Being in an environment that fosters these attributes gives you a huge leg-up. This is not, however, the environment in which Nick himself was fortunate enough to start out.

After finishing a Masters degree in Applied Mathematics, he got his first full-time job in 1993. The project was based on a grand vision; to help the military make their fighter planes invisible to the human eye. As the cold war had just ended, there was less need for military technology on both sides, contracts ceased and as a result Nick lost his job.

To support his family, he helped three different small companies get their websites up and running, adding content and maintaining them. 'I must have been one of the first people in Russia to have had the title of Webmaster,' he recalls.

He later landed a job in an IT development firm that counted the Central Bank of Russia as one of its customers. While there, Nick approached his boss and pitched the idea of developing software that would enable the Russian banks to make transfers amongst each other electronically, efficiently and safely, using what was then the latest web technology. The boss gave him permission to go ahead, and in 1998 the new service was deployed for beta testing in the Central Bank of Russia. A year later, 80% of all transfers between Russian banks were running on this system. It wasn't until 2006 that the system was replaced, and by then it was handling 1 million transactions a day.

But Nick didn't stay put long. By the end of 1999 he was already beginning to get bored, so he took a job as deputy CTO at one of the hottest Russian start-ups at the time, Aport.ru. The new company was a search engine which in 12 months had gone from 10 to 200 employees. Four months later the bubble burst, and despite being in the midst of selling to a strategic investor, Nick's gut told him that there was something wrong with the scenario and that it was time to move on. He rightly followed his gut and, although his instincts were correct, he once again found himself without a job.

This time, however, he felt ready to start out on his own. Together with four former colleagues he launched an IT outsourcing company that made use of the team's expertise within high-performance web solutions. Today, NTR Lab has 50 full-time pro-grammers, and is making so much money that Nick has invested in 8 other start-ups since 2006. One of these has now itself reached a size of 40 employees, coupled with solid growth. Several of the others are well on their way.

As a business angel Nick is by no means conventional. He sees his enterprise as a fusion of an incubator, a venture capital firm and an accelerator programme. He takes an operational role himself in the newest start-ups, which are all, if possible, under the same roof. This particular set-up started randomly, but is what led Nick to one of his most important discoveries. 'When several start-ups sit side-by-side with each other, they begin to cover each others' blind spots. They help each other across the board, because every-body loves to contribute with that something that they do best,' he says.

'In one of my start-ups, there's a guy who's a great salesman. One day the phone rang and he picked it up because the neighbour-ing team was out for lunch. This was a prospective customer and although it wasn't his own start-up, his gut reaction was to use all of his talent to close the deal. Which he did. Back from lunch, there was great joy but also confusion amongst his neighbours, because the introverted programmers had not believed it was possible to sell anything at this point.

'This is just one small example, but it illustrates a mechanism which is extremely strong and effective,' says Nick.

Nick is not alone in his discovery. Incubators got a bad reputation after the first bubble. It became fashionable to work in your garage (or living room) instead of in a room with other entrepreneurs. But why? Yes, the rent is cheap and the garage may have the advantage that a mother, father, wife or husband can easily pop in with a cup of freshly brewed coffee.

But the disadvantages are obvious. Who spots the opportunities that you and your team miss? Who, with a completely different set of skills and perspectives, offers you a spontaneous exchange of experiences? Everything you need to know you can find online, but it requires first that you know that you're missing it. The same applies to contacts and energy. Today we call them accelerator programmes and eager entrepreneurs flock to them by the thousands. Most entrepreneurs dream of being allowed to spend weekends, weeks or months under the same roof as a large group of like-minded people. They know that it creates a momentum that no garage can compete with.

Nick focuses on nurturing this environment, which allows for all those within it to flourish and feed off each other's energy and momentum. For Nick, maximum efficiency is a necessity because he doesn't intend to spend all of his waking hours slaving away in front of his computer screen or attending endless meetings.

'I've experimented and discovered that 60 hours a week is not sustainable for me. I can feel it physically. Weekends are sacred and I spend them with my wife and my three children. In the winter season, I go ski racing in the woods, which is a 5-minute walk from our home on the outskirts of Moscow. Often, I go twice in one day,' Nick says.

Whether it's the fresh air on those skiing trips or the joy of living his passion, 39-year-old Nick looks 10 years younger than he is, and if the road from his native town in Siberia to life as a successful entrepreneur in Moscow has been challenging, then it is not something that has corroded his lust for life or his sense of humour.

EFFICIENCY BOOSTER #5:
PUT YOURSELF IN A HIGH-ENERGY, INSPIRING
ENVIRONMENT WITH OTHER ENTREPRENEURS

#6 STAND OUT

BY MARTIN BJERGEGAARD

In 2002 Torsten Hvidt and four friends began a journey along a road that was uphill, full of obstacles and quite narrow.

At least that's what it may have looked like from the outside. The five of them wanted to provide strategic consultancy for the largest companies in Scandinavia in direct competition with top global consulting empires, whose intellectual capital, track record and number of dinner engagements with Fortune 500 CEOs can send shivers down the spine of any independent strategy consultant with ambitions to do more than feed themselves and their family.

But Torsten and his friends had a secret weapon. They were different. Not more intelligent, diligent or ambitious than their competitors (that's hardly possible) – but different. Inside Torsten's company an expression to describe this characteristic is 'man bites dog', which is also a monthly prize awarded to the team that has delivered the most notable 'bite'. This focus has helped them to grow relatively quickly to a team of 150 successful strategy consultants in offices spread out across Copenhagen, Stockholm and Oslo. On their list of loyal customers are Carlsberg, Maersk, Novo, LEGO and Vestas, Danish companies that have all gone truly global. Customer relationships are so strong that some of these customers have agreed to let the consulting firm's meeting rooms

bear their names and be decorated with items from the clients' daily life. So be ready to play with LEGO or try not to topple over the large model of a can of beer if you one day go to a meeting at Quartz & Co.

Torsten has a wife and four children, to whom he comes home (on most days) at 6 pm. He enjoys frequent holidays with family and friends, and heated discussions about both literature and football. Torsten doesn't like stereotypes and simplified perspectives on life, so I'll refrain from declaring that his life is 'complete' or 'perfect', and shall restrict myself to noting that he has managed to create a highly successful business, while still having time for family, friends and himself.

But what kind of man would bite a dog? That's precisely the question. Imagine you saw a newspaper headline that read 'Dog Bites Man'. Would you buy the newspaper? Hardly. If on the other hand it said 'Man Bites Dog', then it would be far more likely to catch your eye. It is this insight that Torsten and his colleagues have refined and effectively brought into play.

'There has to be an element of "man bites dog" about each assignment we solve,' Torsten explains. 'We expect all our consultants to think creatively, stand out, and create the extraordinary, as opposed to the ordinary. We'll go to great lengths to avoid death by PowerPoint. We're willing to take chances; we've done quite remarkable things in relation to our presentations and task deliveries.'

Torsten tells me of the time they were pitching for a job against the global competitors that dominate the industry. It was about optimisation of logistics, and the project manager had the idea of putting the presentation up on the walls all around the conference room rather than showing it on a screen – as a physical illustration of the points he raised throughout the presentation. 'It was a chance we took; we could have been met with shaking heads. We moved a lot of stuff around in the client's meeting room, and that was even before we'd won the job. But the client accepted the terms, was thrilled, and chose us, in part, because of "the extraordinary". Our fundamental idea is that we must be on a par with the best in the world with regards to the content of our problem solving – but better in form and energy,' Torsten says.

Quartz & Co. take their own medicine, and are different on the inside as well. For example, they have no titles in their company. 'Our hierarchies are situational; the leader is the one who has followership in that specific situation. We're all leaders sometimes and followers other times; we call it lead and be led,' says Torsten. Also, there's no one in Quartz & Co. who has their own office or parking space. Not even the owners.

The reward for idiosyncracies is easy to spot: Quartz & Co. is a talent magnet. 'We've never used traditional job postings. People have come to us, because they are attracted to the way we are,' Torsten says.

The idea of being different is not new. In 2002 Seth Godin wrote the bestseller *Purple Cow* to make us understand that a purple cow, and everything else that is strange, has a better chance of attracting attention in marketing – and the idea has probably existed ever since the first Neanderthal suddenly started trimming his hair, greatly shocking or amusing his more conventional friends.

In many ways, however, we are still far too similar. When Derek Sivers got the idea to write a funny 'thank you for your order' email to customers in his web-shop CD Baby, he was one of the first to do it, and for it he received a lot of attention and goodwill. But why had no one thought of it before? Why had thousands of online shops carried on copying and pasting the same boring and humourless standard emails into their system? Probably because we humans are gregarious animals and like to follow the crowd. That's how we survive, and in many ways it's a fine quality. But it also means that you have enormous opportunities to make your company stand out in a business landscape that is basically eerily conformist.

Thought-provoking:

- Why are there tables and chairs in all meeting rooms?
- Why are all physical books (including this one) rectangular and printed on paper?
- Why do all stores put up their Christmas decorations in December?
- Why do all men in the financial sector wear a tie?
- Why do no entrepreneurs in Silicon Valley wear a tie?
- When was the last time you did something that was so different it made other people stop and notice it?

EFFICIENCY BOOSTER #6:
ALWAYS LOOK FOR WAYS TO STAND OUT

#7 LEVERAGE TECHNOLOGY

BY JORDAN MILNE

As you read these pages, scores of the brightest people around the world are working intensely to develop solutions that will make your life easier.

From Silicon Valley to Seattle to New York, from London to Munich to Tokyo, millions of innovative talents are focusing their immense energy into developing greater and more efficient technologies, putting clever ideas into practice and changing the way we live and work. Their efforts are helping you to communicate more seamlessly, work more efficiently and learn more quickly. In short: they are working to make your life just that little bit easier.

Of course, they may be in it for the money, but they are also here to help. They even have teams dedicated to making sure you hear about what they've been up to (marketing), giving it to you at a reasonable price (sales) and showing you how to use it (support). And for many products, they even have full teams on board to make sure these innovations look nice and make you feel good when you hold them in your hands and show them off to your friends (design).

And what is the role most of us play in this process of innovation? Simply to pick and choose which of those brilliant innovations we think will help us most. Then we go to the shop and pick one up or sign up for a subscription online. Not a bad deal.

Although we are not yet riding around in hover cars or teleporting from one side of the planet to another, we do have some very impressive technologies at our fingertips. Everything from Internet connectivity in the palm of our hand to free global calls at the touch of a button and drinking a beer on our iPhone (yes, there is an app for that). **For those on the quest to live a balanced life, leveraging IT can be one piece of the puzzle**.

Sophie Vandebroek, CTO of XEROX, knows this and leverages technology to its fullest.

'Leveraging IT allows you to do so much more outside of the physical office as well as within the traditional 9–5. You don't have to be at work to write your papers, do your analysis or make presentations. Many people believe face time is important. To me it was always what you delivered that is important. Throughout my career I've done a lot of work from home, which has always given me the opportunity to really enjoy both work and home. For example, today I'm doing my quarterly communication from home. I have a simple big screen. It's not an expensive installation – just the next level up from Skype. I use it to talk to all of my team from around the world – from my home office,' says Sophie.

There are countless examples of how technology has made the life of an entrepreneur easier.

Making a simple market test is now faster than ever before. With the likes of WordPress you can get an online presence for your business in days, if not hours or even minutes.

Marketing campaigns using YouTube, if harnessed correctly (and with a little bit of luck), can reach millions in record time. For those who know how to use it, exposure is available at levels previously unheard of. Not 10 years ago a company would have had to run a multimillion dollar marketing campaign to see results half the size of those obtained now by a couple of bright kids with their video-phone. Who would have thought the 'Bed Intruder Song' would have reached 80 million views and spawned a hit single on iTunes? And who would have thought possible the national media attention surrounding the 'Double Rainbow' video?

Daily engagement with your audience and customers is now commonplace as Twitter easily allows you to spread the word more effectively. Working together has also never been easier – managing projects with Basecamp, sharing files seamlessly with DropBox and connecting with your co-workers using Yammer or HipChat. Looking to synch your computer screen with that of one of your colleagues? Teamview has you covered. Doodle saves you a headache when organising meetings with multiple partners. When used in the right way, technology can make things flow.

So when you are looking for a solution to make life a little bit easier, remember all those bright minds working passionately to help you solve your problem.

EFFICIENCY BOOSTER #7:

ALLOW THE NEW IT TOOLS AND TECHNOLOGIES

TO DO SOME OF YOUR WORK FOR YOU

#8 PUT PEOPLE FIRST

BY MARTIN BJERGEGAARD

What is the difference between the mediocre leader who works his or her ass off, yet never really makes it big, and the leader who achieves amazing results, with apparent ease and without making huge sacrifices to get there?

A critical component of that answer is **the ability to engage with the right people, to motivate and inspire them, and to create the right kind of culture**. We all know this answer, but getting there is a long journey for most of us.

This is where we need the advice of Henrik Lind. Henrik is the creator of Danske Commodities, Lind Finans, and a number of other successful companies, making him one of the most successful entrepreneurs in Denmark. During the last 3 years his businesses have enjoyed a combined pre-tax profit of more than $100 million. Quite an achievement considering that he has only been an entrepreneur for 7 years, and that he has built his business empire from scratch.

Given that he has so many different companies and such a high rate of success, you are probably picturing Henrik as some kind of ego-driven workaholic. This, however, couldn't be further from the truth. Henrik grew up in a perfectly average family in a small countryside town. He is down-to-earth and family oriented, enjoying life with his wife and three children.

On a typical day, Henrik arrives home around 5 pm, giving him plenty of time to play with his children before tucking them up for the night. Because his family is his top priority he keeps his travelling to a minimum, setting out only a couple of days each month. He is the one who gets the kids ready for school every morning and is, just as often as his wife, the one they call out for when they wake up at night and need comforting.

Henrik can teach us a lot about both success and happiness. In our interview he starts by focusing on the one area he considers the most important to his success, an area in which he always makes sure he is generous with his time: his all-too-important interactions with his colleagues.

'As CEO of Danske Commodities I was present at every single job interview the company conducted and at every one of our employees' evaluation meetings. It took quite a bit of time, because we did quarterly evaluations, but in my view, it was the most important thing I could spend my time on. It meant clear communications and a harmonisation of expectations between new employees and us. It also meant that we agreed on goals and responsibilities with each individual colleague and reinforced our culture,' Henrik tells us. 'We have an amazing culture at Danske Commodities. Everyone is motivated, takes responsibility and puts in an honest effort. With so many talented people, the company can move quickly and I never become the bottleneck,' he continues.

Henrik truly puts people first and at the office he spends most of his time being accessible and available for his colleagues. They can always bounce a new idea off him, ask for advice or tell him about their plans. Recently he got a new CEO on board, and is now in the process of getting used to his new role as chairman.

Henrik goes on: 'In our company the value of the argument is more important than who presents it. Even our recent graduates would come to me with great ideas and I would give them the leeway to carry them out. I have the mindset that if people come to me, it's probably because they feel I can somehow contribute.'

At first it might seem inefficient to spend so much time on internal meetings and conversation. However, in reality, it is actually the very reason that Henrik can take time off to be with his family.

He has created a team that can function by itself, and he sustains that culture through compassionate leadership made possible by his presence and sincere interest in those he works with. How many leaders and entrepreneurs can honestly say they are doing the same? This is an area where stepping up can give most of us a huge efficiency boost.

EFFICIENCY BOOSTER #8:
MAKE SURE YOU SPEND ENOUGH TIME
WITH YOUR TEAM

#9 INTERACT WITH THE ENERGY OF OTHERS

BY MARTIN BJERGEGAARD

Quantum physicists describe the universe as a giant tapestry of energy. They claim that the objective world doesn't contain colour or form, is not ugly or beautiful, but simply consists of energy. For most well-grounded entrepreneurs this concept may be too abstract, but most of us acknowledge that interrelated energy is a reality.

A good starting point, to benefit from and contribute to this universal weave of energy, is to optimise your own. We have already spoken about following your own energy, but no matter how energised you become, you are still just one person in a very big world. One thread in the tapestry. **To accomplish something significant, you have to allow your own energy to interact with the energy of others**.

For months and even years I had thought about writing this book, yet nothing worth mentioning happened. Then I met Jordan. Our energy interacted as he shared my passion for the field and, just like me, had already penned a collection of notes and thoughts. We agreed to write a book together. With this partnership, the ball started rolling. Everything that I had previously been unable to get done by myself suddenly became a fun and playful process with Jordan on board.

Something that practically all our role models share is that they have understood and utilised this principle. They create ideas, visions and momentum in interaction with others, in turn increasing their bandwidth exponentially. The total becomes larger than the sum of the parts. We feel more dedicated when someone else is as passionate about a project as we are. Often in the process of writing this book, there were lulls when I hadn't written anything. The catalyst for getting at it again was an email from Jordan with his latest essay.

Chad Troutwine experienced a similar phenomenon with his company Veritas Prep. When he and his co-founder, Markus Moberg, met at The Yale School of Management they began working on Chad's idea together.

Early on Chad made clear his intention himself to pursue the venture full time. At this point Markus was entertaining opportunities on Wall Street; however, Chad knew that Markus's energy would be a huge asset in bringing the project forward. The two sat down to dinner one night and Chad asked Markus to become a full and equal partner. He convinced Markus to forego a position on Wall Street in order to join him. From there on things escalated.

Chad and Markus fed off each other's energy as well as depending on one another every day. This partnership is what has given them the strength to build what is today one of the preeminent test preparations companies in the world, making both of them multimillionaires in the process. This partnership is also what gives them the flexibility and peace of mind to pursue balanced lifestyles. This energy, this give and take, and the fact that Chad and Markus's combined energy is so great, is what makes it work.

As soon as you have an idea that you want to explore, make it a habit to immediately ask yourself: 'Who would also have a passion for this project?' Call up that person, meet over a cup of coffee and see if the right energy emerges. This is the quickest way to move forward.

EFFICIENCY BOOSTER # 9:
HOOK UP WITH PEOPLE WHO SHARE
YOUR PASSION

#10 MASTER THE ART OF LISTENING

BY MARTIN BJERGEGAARD

Bill Liao – a successful Australian entrepreneur and philanthropist now living in Ireland – is an unusual man with an unusual approach to success: he listens.

Success is something he has in spades, both as a human being and in the business world. He possesses a rare blend of calm and charisma, and laughs cheerfully, reminding me many times of the Dalai Lama during our conversation. Perhaps it is not purely a coincidence. Just as His Holiness has achieved incredible results, so has Liao, seemingly without obsessing about it.

Liao has been a driving force in seven IPOs, including XING.com: a social network for professionals, which in 2006 became the first European Web 2.0 start-up to go public. In 2009 Germany's Burda Media Group bought 25% of XING, valuing the company at $287 million. Today Liao is an investor, philanthropist, author and speaker. As a co-founder of the venture capital firm SOS Ventures, he has invested in a wide range of prominent projects, including TechStars and 500 Startups. He has set himself a mission of planting two trillion trees by 2020, and has set up the NGO WeForrest.org for this purpose. The counter on the website shows that the first 983,993 trees are in the ground and are helping to offset human CO_2 emissions. CO_2 weighs heavily on Liao's mind. He once got a ride to the USA on a cargo ship. It took 3 weeks to get there, but the trip was 100% environmentally neutral. The trip also gave Liao plenty of time to think along the way.

When asked about his secret, he answers: 'The key to my success is to listen. I listen with my ears, with my intuition and with my entire body. When I speak, I listen with my eyes and my senses at the same time. I am always listening.'

'**The answer to many difficult situations is to be quiet**,' Liao continues – but only when I ask him to. 'Whether it is to close a deal or resolve a conflict with my wife. I knew a used car salesman named Vac in Queensland, Australia, who used to say to me; "In every sale there is a moment of golden silence. The first person to talk owns a very nice car." Vac was something as rare as an honest car salesman, and he sold more cars than any of his colleagues. His method was to create an initial interest, build up trust, deal with the customer's objections, and at just the right moment ask: "So how about we write this up for you?" Then he would nod gently, smile a bit, hold the customer's eyes, and wait – continue to wait.'

Listening can generate sales. So far, so good. But what about management, I ask Liao.

'I once had a colleague who suddenly changed dramatically for the worse. She had started a new relationship with a guy who was breaking her down. Deep down she knew it, but it had not yet settled in her own mind. If I had started talking, telling her that she was in a dysfunctional relationship, how do you think she would have reacted? She would have probably left the company rather than the guy. Instead, I asked questions and listened to her while she talked herself out of the relationship. She went home and broke up with him, and returned to being her usual happy self, as well as a good colleague,' is the answer I get.

You might think Bill Liao has developed some incredibly intelligent questions. But the beauty is in the simplicity of his favourite three:

- Tell me more about that
- Does that make sense?
- What does that mean to you?

'Your questions don't need to be carefully thought out,' says Liao. 'The hard part is to keep quiet and resist the temptation to give advice.'

We open up when we're listened to. On the other hand we close up, become defensive or argumentative when we're faced with judgments and opinions. This we've heard before, but why is it so important to listen when you, like us entrepreneurs, are full of visions and ideas, and really just want to put them into practice?

'The secret of growing a successful company is growing great people. The way you do that is to listen to them,' is Bill Liao's simple answer.

If it's crucially important to listen, how can it be that so many of us have such difficulties doing it? Most often we are listening only in anticipation of our own answer. We are looking for breaks in the flow of speech so that we can interrupt and offer our own views on the matter.

'We all have an ego, and quite often we try to please it, instead of trying to grasp what is going on inside the mind of the person we are talking to. The key is to be present. When we are consumed by thoughts our ego becomes dangerous, but when we are fully present the ego is just a flavouring, and we can listen without judgement,' Liao tells me.

But what about situations where we become agitated, angry or even feel threatened? Surely it isn't reasonable to expect that we can remain calm and just listen?

'It is important to bear in mind how our brain works. In the face of danger the primal part of our brain, the limbic system, will always kick in first. It doesn't matter how enlightened you are; if you stub your toes, you curse. The trick is to realise it and get back to being a human being as fast as you can. Our primitive brain cannot distinguish an attack on our physical body from an attack on our point of view. Whereas the right solution might very well be fight or flight in the case of a physical attack, it produces much better results to keep your cool and listen in the case of verbal aggression,' Liao explains.

'Even in a crowded room, if you listen intently, other people will start listening too. If people get hotter and hotter because of some disagreement, try to notice how their arguments get more and more simplistic as their temperatures rise. In those cases I always choose to listen instead of adding to the disputes. What you then finally say after having listened intensely for a while can easily be far more intelligent than anything else that is being said at that time. Keeping your own cool, however, is the real challenge. The method? Have compassion. Compassion is a very powerful way to stay calm.'

After the interview, I realise that I am impressed. Impressed by the points, but even more by the way Bill Liao embodied them throughout our conversation. Despite the fact that I was the interviewer, I had felt listened to. I had felt understood, and I had felt like talking to Bill again. I wanted to know him better, to work with him and to learn from him.

The next time I feel the urge to open my mouth and say something, I intend to ask myself first: is there, in this situation, a greater call for me as a speaker or as a listener?

EFFICIENCY BOOSTER #10:
LISTEN INTENTLY TO HONESTLY
UNDERSTAND THE OTHER'S PERSPECTIVE

#11 MAKE YOURSELF LEAN

BY MARTIN BJERGEGAARD

My grandfather, Valdemar Rønne Jensen, lived from 1921 to 2002. He grew up in dire circumstances as the youngest in a family of nine children, where money was always scarce. He once told me how he and his siblings, in especially rough times, would be sent out to steal chickens from their better-off but unfortunately stingy uncle so that they would have food on the table.

High school education wasn't something there was time or money for, so Valde soon started working at the local factory. Every worker was assigned a workstation with a machine tool they used to produce different pieces made in the factory. The machine tool was called a lathe and was versatile in that it could perform several operations depending on what kind of piece had to be produced. From his lathe Valde had a view of dozens of colleagues who, like him, were considered worth less than the tools they were using. 'A worker is a 10-cent stamp,' the factory owner used to remind his employees, referring to the amount it cost to send a letter to the employment office asking them to send a new worker to the factory the following morning.

The work at the lathe was piecework; Valde and the others received a specific amount of money for each unit they produced. At a time and within a social class where the household budget was only barely enough to make it through the day, this was the perfect method to make all the workers sign in on Monday morning with the same unrelenting focus which characterises a boxer on his way into the ring to face a terrifying opponent. The second after they had signed in, they threw themselves at the lathe so as to, as quickly as possible, get the first pieces in the box they had to fill.

My grandfather, however, was different. He had his own method. At the factory, many products were manufactured and the change to a new product happened every Monday. Valde took his time. He spent every Monday adjusting his lathe, optimising and experimenting with the order of his movements, so he could design the most efficient process from beginning to end. For him, Monday was reserved to think carefully about the job ahead and plan it just right. Unlike the others, for Valde there was no hectic activity at the lathe and no finished pieces in his box, only experiments and reflection.

Among many of his friends and colleagues on the floor there was a high degree of solidarity, and the others watched with worry out of the corners of their eyes at how Valde 'wasted' all of his Monday. Their thoughts probably went to Valde's wife, Ruth, who came from the middle class, and for whom just any standard of living wouldn't do. Or to little Allan, my father, who needed new clothes as he grew.

But Valde was calm. He knew what he was doing. On Tuesday, Wednesday and Thursday he could, without difficulty, match his colleagues' production for an entire week. His movements were precise and his tools were a continuation of his hands. Piece after piece piled up by his small workstation. His colleagues did not know it, but what they were witnessing was an early example of 'lean', the principle pioneered by Toyota that looks to optimise all key processes.

Today, many have discovered how powerful the philosophy and methods of lean can be. In my grandfather's time few had yet realised its potential.

Armed with his first success, Valde increased the application of his method. After he had reached the weekly quota for production on Thursday, he spent his Friday helping those of his colleagues who were behind. That made him spokesperson, first for his floor and later for the whole factory. He became an active union member and after a couple of years he earned a permanent appointment in the union office, where he rose in the ranks to the respected job of treasurer. He worked to improve the system's efficiency, gave the unemployment fund what he called 'a human face' and, to cut a long story short, became a well-known and respected man in his town.

He also bought an estate on the outskirts of town, where his son Allan later built his own house. This beautiful place, called Valhal, became my childhood home where I shared a happy upbringing with my family and spent a great deal of time with my grandfather. My grandfather still stands as one of the greatest role models in my life. Not because he understood lean before most others, but because he had the courage to do things his own way, and because, in a very concrete way, he illustrated to me how you can make a good life for yourself while also helping others.

It is easy enough to believe that lean is something that is relevant only to factories or for office workers who repeat the same process again and again. But the reality is that **all of us can greatly increase our efficiency by sizing up the tasks we are faced with well ahead of time so as to design an effective plan of attack**.

For example, when we buy a new gadget the natural thing for most of us is to dive right in and learn how to make do along the way. Instead, we should probably spend some time simply learning the features properly, so that we can maximise our efficiency using the equipment tomorrow and the day after.

Likewise, when we choose a CRM or accounting software, we are often impatient to get the preparatory work over with, so we can start sending emails to customers or issuing invoices. But in all likelihood we will be using this program for a long time to come, so even if it may take an entire week to find the best program to fit our needs, that week would be well spent.

When you began using Facebook, did you spend a morning adjusting your preferences to fit your needs and getting to know all the possibilities? Or was your approach like mine: 'Let me get this thing working as quickly as possible, so I can invite some friends who can read my first status update'?

Have you configured your email program to automatically place all incoming emails in the right folders? Do you still email documents or pictures back and forth or have you signed up to use online file sharing systems such as Flick'r and Google docs?

Of course efficient processes aren't only about choosing the right IT systems. If you are cold calling, have you spent a day preparing with someone more experienced in that field than you? And did you experiment with five different openings, question frameworks and ending remarks to find out which strategies work best on different types of people? Have you made a system in your closet that ensures you don't waste 10 minutes every morning searching for the right outfit for the day?

While improvisation is important, systematic thinking can be our best friend. Even though we are entrepreneurs and no two days are alike, there are lots of processes we repeat over and over again. Making presentations, analysing data and going to meetings, to name just three. Have you thought through, experimented with and optimised the 20 most important and recurrent processes in your life? If not, the best thing you can do for your efficiency is very likely to let yourself find inspiration in the story of my grandfather and reserve every Monday during the next month to get started on implementing 'lean' in your own life.

> ## EFFICIENCY BOOSTER #11:
> ## APPLY THE LEAN APPROACH TO
> ## YOUR DAILY ACTIVITIES

#12 DON'T TRY TOO HARD

Have you ever noticed how the most successful people seem far more relaxed than the rest of us, even though in theory they should be far more stressed? How the president exudes a calm and collected demeanour, while all his helpers look hectic?

This was the case, almost universally, when we interviewed our role models. None of them seemed stressed despite running large, successful businesses or disruptive start-ups.

One possible explanation for their impressively calm demeanour could be that since they have already achieved so much they can now rest a little on their laurels. In reality, however, the causality points the other way: they have come so far, exactly because they possess the skill of being relaxed in the midst of hectic activity.

It may seem unnatural that the road to success should be paved with relaxation. I know that for me this was initially a very difficult notion to accept. I thought about all the times I had done a good job by pushing myself.

My mindset changed only when martial arts champion, bestselling author and meditation teacher Henning Daverne asked me to think of the situations when I had done my absolute best. My true

EFFICIENCY BOOSTERS / 65

personal top performances. I then realised that there is a limit to what I can achieve by pushing myself. The performances I'm most proud of have all happened in a state of flow and ease, at the point where everything comes together and I perform well above my normal level. That's what Henning calls effortless drive, and he knows what he's talking about.

Henning's own breakthrough as a fighter came when he himself learned how to relax. It was in 1989, at a rally in Sweden. He was up against a strong fighter, a real ox. The two young men battled and struggled, crashed together and spent enormous amounts of energy on their efforts to defeat each other. Henning realised that he couldn't win by sheer muscle alone, and changed his strategy.

He began to relax, to breathe deeply, and to distance himself from his situation and his opponent. He observed it all calmly, both from inside and above. And then bang, he landed a perfect blow. Because all his effort had been replaced with presence and tranquillity, it became easy for Henning to respond intuitively, without hesitation and without having to push himself. The battle was won, and Henning continued to use the principle to become one of the most highly ranked Wing Tsun practitioners in Europe.

Do you know the salesman who's so eager to get the contract that the whole sale crumbles between his tightly clenched fingers? Or the young consultant who so desperately wants to do well that she turns the entire department against her?

In caricatured form it is easy to laugh at or pity these unfortunate people, but the reality is that, now and then, we are all that person. We are trying so hard to achieve a result that we fail.

Through effortless drive you not only get better results, but you also wear yourself down less in the process. An extra benefit is that the transition from one activity to another becomes much easier when you are less uptight.

EFFICIENCY BOOSTER #12:
RELAX AND ENJOY THE PROCESS

#13 RIDE THE WAVE

BY JORDAN MILNE

Not only can you see it coming, you can also feel it. The undertow moves beneath you and then the current shifts. You paddle quickly. Anticipation mounts. You can hear the water. Suddenly you're moving swiftly and begin to accelerate. You paddle a few more times. Hard. Your heart beats faster. In one final motion you feel the power of the water underneath you and you begin to stand up on the board. And then the moment comes … there is nothing like catching a wave. Everything comes together. You glide effortlessly along the water, carving turns. You feel the power beneath you. You don't know how long it will last, but it's exhilarating. When the water finally melts onto the surf you feel lucky to have caught the wave.

Sometimes working can be a struggle. You arrive at the office in the morning and never really get into the flow. You open up tasks and labour through them, forcing yourself to work on something simply because it's what's in front of you. You feel like you are just treading water on your board. Get into the office early, leave late. Rinse. Repeat.

Then there are times when everything clicks. You simply feel on. Writing your proposal just flows. A task that should take hours takes 20 minutes. Jason Fried knows this feeling and knows how to get it more often. Jason knows how to ride the wave.

Fried is truly a revolutionary entrepreneur. He is well respected in his industry, not only for his products but also for his process. He marches to his own beat and challenges the status quo. His style of business is unorthodox, and the world is taking notice. His book *REWORK* is an international bestseller.

Jason Fried is the founder of 37 Signals, a Chicago-based company he launched in 1999 along with Ernest Kin and Carlos Segura. The company started as a web design firm, but fate had other plans. In 2003, a Danish programmer named David Heinemeier was brought onto the team to write software to bring order to the company's many design projects. The collaboration software itself quickly became popular among clients. So popular, in fact, that in 2005 the company began completely focusing on the development of web applications. 37 Signals now boasts some of the best tools to make collaborative working easier – tools such as Basecamp, Highrise and Campfire – and has millions of customers. Now generating multimillion dollar profits, 37 Signals must be doing something right.

The company is self-funded, except for one angel investor. Count-less others have tried to get on board, but only one investor was able to make the cut: Jeff Bezos, founder of Amazon.

What is perhaps even more remarkable about Jason Fried is that he is truly balanced. He is happy, enjoys his life and works less than 40 hours per week.

While many entrepreneurs struggle to complete their daily tasks,

Jason is cheerfully progressing. How does he do it? How does Jason work productively and enjoy what he's doing, feeling invigorated, instead of overwhelmed? How does he catch the wave?

One key lies in Jason's philosophy of choosing what he works on and when. He listens to his energy levels and works accordingly. He is flexible and works with his body and mind instead of always obeying the clock.

'It's about asking, what do I feel I'd be good at right now? If I'm not feeling creative right now I probably shouldn't do something creative just because I'm at work. I should be doing what I feel like doing. Sometimes that's paying the bills, sometimes it's writing a letter. It could be anything. It doesn't matter what time it is or where I am, when I feel the energy to do something I do it,' Jason explains to me on our Skype call.

Forget 9 to 5. Work the hours that are best for you and set out to do the tasks that give you energy at that moment. By being flexible as well as in tune with your own energy levels you can catch more waves. **When you feel an energy wave coming, get yourself into a position to capitalise on it**. Be flexible and keep asking yourself 'what do I feel I'd be good at right now?' And then do that. You will surely get that done much more quickly and on a higher level than something you are forcing yourself to do. By flowing with your energy levels instead of fighting them you can be more efficient. People have energy at different times of the day. Different cycles. Find out what your best schedule is and tune into your body's energy levels.

Design your own life; don't live by conventions.

EFFICIENCY BOOSTER #13:
DARE TO FOLLOW YOUR ENERGY

#14 BUILD YOUR BRAIN

BY MARTIN BJERGEGAARD

A violin player has a brain that is different from yours. Researchers have demonstrated that our brain gets shaped according to the way we use it, just as our physical muscles are affected by whether we're desk-bound or climbing mountains.

Violin players use the left ring finger for several hours each day, and as a result they form more neural connections in the part of the brain that controls that particular finger. CT scans of violin players show that this area of their brain actually grows because of playing the violin. Most teens today don't play the violin, but use their right thumb for texting, whereas the rest of us used our voices at that age. Like playing the violin, sending a few hundred text messages a day also leaves an imprint on the shape of the brain.

Just as you can train your brain to play the violin or send text messages, you can also decide for yourself how good you want to be at making decisions, devising creative solutions and acting in social contexts. These skills are created in your prefrontal cortex (among other places), side by side with your ability to enjoy life and feel inner peace.

Not a bad area to develop.

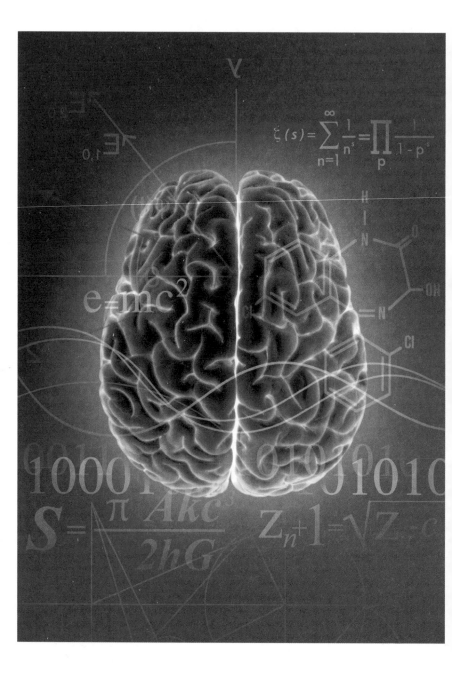

Using brain scans, researchers have identified what activities best stimulate this part of the brain. Near the top of almost all the studies is one particular activity: meditation.

Researchers have known for many years that meditation can cause positive changes in the brain, based on scans of practitioners who had meditated at least 45 minutes a day for at least 10 years. Their brain area of both happiness and complex problem-solving was much larger than those in the control group.

Forty-five minutes a day is a long time, and for those of us who want to achieve a lot in every dimension of our lives, it may seem like an impossible investment in brain training. Because we already use our brains a lot, many of us might feel more like going out for a run than spending 45 minutes in the lotus position after finishing work.

So how little time spent meditating is really enough to make an impact? This is a question meditation teacher, speaker, bestselling author and former professional martial artist Henning Daverne (whom we met on page 65) asked himself and the Danish brain researcher Troels W. Kjær. The results of their study are described in their recent book *12 Minutes to Success – Meditate Yourself Wiser, Calmer and Happier*. It turns out that at 12 minutes a day there is a breakthrough in the brain in which new neural connections are created, thus augmenting your ability for intimacy, concentration and collaboration. The results are visible on brain scans after approximately 2 months, and must be maintained in order to enjoy the full advantage.

During meditation, the production of the happiness hormones dopamine, serotonin and oxytocin is increased. At the same time there is a reduction in the formation of adrenaline and cortisol, stress hormones that can be useful 'in the heat of battle', but that we must take regular breaks from. If we don't get these much-needed pauses, our immune system weakens and our memory gets poorer. We get a sense of burnout or perhaps mental restlessness (is your leg shaking right now?).

Think of it as mental capital. **By meditating, you withdraw your loans from the past and the future and allow yourself to invest all of your presence in the moment**. You know them when you see them: people who impress you by being fully and totally present.

The benefits of meditation include: greater mental capacity, reduced stress and an increased sense of joy.

Before an important meeting, a crucial decision, or a difficult task, the most effective thing you can do is to meditate for even 5 minutes. During the next hour you spend working you will be at least 10% more efficient, thus giving you an immediate positive return. At the same time you get to enjoy all of your activities much more because you have prepared yourself to engage in them fully.

EFFICIENCY BOOSTER #14:
MEDITATE FOR 12 MINUTES A DAY

#15 GET YOUR SLEEP

BY JORDAN MILNE

The clients are getting impatient. The door finally swings open and the chairman stumbles into the boardroom. He grabs a banana from the fruit basket, peels it and then proceeds to wash it in a cup of water. He then turns to address the clients with a slurred 'misshheer Rosheester, lesss get down to bushinessss'. You wouldn't go into work drunk, but research has proven that sleep deprivation manifests many of the same symptoms as overconsumption of alcohol. And how many times have we as entrepreneurs pushed through our workday tired?

Thomas Balkin at The Walter Reed Army Institute of Research states that sleep loss leads to deactivation of parts of the brain. More specifically he says that the prefrontal cortex, which is responsible for higher-level thought, and the thalamus, which processes and relays information from the senses, are particularly affected.

According to the International Society for Human Rights (ISHR), sleep deprivation is regarded as torture under international law and is branded as such by the United Nations. The ISHR has clarified that ongoing sleep deprivation leads to a breakdown of the nervous system and to other serious physical and psychological damage. So when you're trying to build the next Google and you are burning the midnight oil, you may want to think again.

Studies from The Mayo Foundation for Medical Education and Research have also cited slowed reaction time, psychiatric problems, obesity, poor immune system function and increased risk and severity of long-term diseases such as high blood pressure, heart disease, diabetes and memory loss as potential direct results of sleep deprivation. In a study on ageing, Professor Eve Van Cauter found that the metabolic and endocrine hormonal changes resulting from a significant sleep debt mimic the hallmarks of ageing. With so much evidence pointing in its favour it simply makes sense to get those couple of extra hours' sleep. Some say you can sleep when you are dead. The irony is, if you employ this strategy that day may come a little sooner than you think.

On Wednesday 21 October 2009 a news story – and a precautionary tale – shook India and the world. The CEO of SAP India, Ranjan Das, passed away as a result of a massive heart attack at 42 years of age. A graduate of Harvard and MIT, Ranjan was an accomplished, seemingly healthy man who exercised regularly, ran marathons and was scrupulous in his eating habits. However, Mr Das routinely slept only 4 hours a day, something not uncommon in entrepreneurs and business leaders. It is now a well-documented fact that sleep deprivation leads to higher risk of heart attack. Signs of this trend in big business are emerging more often. In another widely publicised case, in December 2011, British banking giant Lloyds Banking Group's CEO, Horta-Osario, had to take a two-month medical leave due to exhaustion and a stress-related sleeping disorder. Even if it doesn't shorten your life, lack of sleep affects the quality and efficiency of the time you do have. By staying up those extra few hours on a regular basis your ability to enjoy the things around you, as well as your ability to make business decisions, will be diminished. **If your life was a pier being built into the ocean, sleep would be the foundation pillar holding everything else up**.

The good news is that you can turn sleep deprivation around. Daniel Kripke of the Scripps Clinic Sleep Center in California found that those who sleep between 6.5 and 7.5 hours per night live the longest. These results were supported by similar studies around the globe. Many also suggest that the hours before midnight are more beneficial that those afterwards. For many of us, sleeping an hour longer per night is the best business decision we can make. It sure feels better too.

EFFICIENCY BOOSTER #15:
MAKE BEING FULLY RESTED A KEY PRIORITY

New Ways of Doing Old Things

→ 5 ADJUSTMENTS WITH PROFOUND IMPACT

Some things we do very often, perhaps more often than we would like. Like updating our to-do list, setting up meetings or following online news streams. Each of these are small activities, but when combined they end up consuming a big part of our time and energy, and as a result are often the theme of lectures or training sessions about efficiency.

Most of us have learned a lot about meetings, to-do lists and other activities that fall into this category. But for some reason the most essential opportunities for improvement have slipped under the radar. It's as if we have been focusing on the pennies only to discover we have forgotten the pounds.

In the following section our role models reveal a set of more radical adjustments that can offer you a profound impact. Try, for instance, to completely pause your mind for a minute before reading on – if you don't know how to do that, you will get a new tool to use, every day, in just a few pages.

#1 REINVENT THE MEETING

BY MARTIN BJERGEGAARD

I often wonder how it came to be the unwritten standard for all meetings to happen with everyone seated in chairs huddled around a table. If you had a penchant for conspiracy theories, you might suspect that furniture manufacturers in the infancy of the information age were lobbying corporate leaders and interior designers with beautiful pictures, soft-seat cushions and promises of kickback agreements. But what's really going on here?

For most of human history, it has been otherwise. Farmers talked while working in the fields, hunters as they shared the kill of the day, and fishermen while standing on their boats, gazing out over the sea. **Who taught us that we can only think, communicate and collaborate if we sit down on our behinds, place a table between us, and close the door to the meeting room?**

Claus Meyer – a prolific Danish gastronomic entrepreneur – has a different approach. Claus is the kind of man who wants the most out of life. While studying at the Copenhagen Business School he was also working as a cook at a small restaurant in central Copenhagen. That year, the young Claus persuaded the school president to let him run the business school canteen. Claus had just returned from a year living with a chef and confectioner family in France to find himself inspired and quite sure he had found his calling. He wanted to change the Danish food culture.

The contrast between the first 19 years of his life spent in the culinary darkness of suburban Denmark and the light he saw in France laid the foundation for what would later become a food empire.

Today his businesses have more than 500 employees. They span delis, bakeries, fruit cultivation, gourmet food production, culinary courses and catering, as well as half-ownership of Noma, which is now, for the second year running, named as the best restaurant in the world.

Along the way, Claus became a renowned TV chef in Denmark and got his international breakthrough as the host of the television show *New Scandinavian Cooking*, which has so far been shown in 100 countries and viewed by more than 50 million people.

Claus has an inspiring philosophy for meetings. 'I turn as many meetings as possible into walking or running meetings, especially if we're going to discuss difficult topics. I once walked around Copenhagen in the snow for 2 hours with a colleague. It was a really difficult subject and a fantastic experience.'

When Claus trained for the Berlin Marathon in 2003 he needed lots of exercise. With 12 companies, 500 employees and 3 children he had to think creatively in order to fit it in. 'I need 6 hours of sleep to function properly, and being with my family is very important to me. So I searched my calendar for slots that could be used for exercise. Suddenly it seemed obvious: there were lots of internal meetings with people who are active, like me, that could be turned into training – without harming family, effectiveness or colleagues,' says Claus.

Actually, it's quite simple: our brain works best when our body is in motion. That's why we rarely get our best ideas sitting in a chair. Sharing an activity also creates a connection between people and is an optimal starting point for mutual understanding. A table between us, on the other hand, creates distance, and a closed door makes the atmosphere formal and inhibits creativity. When sitting you get less blood to the brain, and as the meeting progresses, many of us can become distracted and sluggish, maybe even irritable or disengaged.

There are, of course, some conditions that must be met for holding an effective meeting while on the run. Claus explains, 'Before we go out into the streets of Copenhagen, we arrange the topics we will discuss and agree what we want to accomplish from the meeting. If necessary, we will take notes with our smart phones along the way. We choose activities we are all comfortable doing, such as walking, running or rollerblading.'

I personally didn't discover this strategy until I was pushed into it. I was preparing for a very challenging meeting, and my intuition told me that I wouldn't get through the session successfully if we sat on chairs inside a meeting room. So we held the meeting while walking, and the outcome exceeded all my expectations.

It was still a difficult meeting, but I managed to get my message across with the best possible empathy and precision.

Since that day 3 years ago, I have used walking, running and cycling meetings regularly. Walking meetings are especially easy, because they require no change of clothes – all we have to do is to go downstairs and out into the street instead of into the conference room.

We have a beautiful park near the office. Previously, I would sometimes get a little sad looking out of the window and seeing one of those rare but captivating Danish summer days when I was trapped inside with a packed calendar. Thankfully, this is no longer the case.

ADJUSTMENT #1:
TAKE WALKING, RUNNING OR
BIKING MEETINGS

#2 MAKE A 'TODAY' LIST

One of the potentials of entrepreneurship as opposed to other jobs is freedom. People long for flexible work hours, afternoons off and the ability to pick up and leave to do something fun at the drop of a hat:

'I could set my own schedule.'

'I could work from the beach or from the skyscrapers in Tokyo.'

'I could pack up and travel the world.'

As you have probably noticed, the path to reaching that dream is tantalisingly difficult for the vast majority of those who try. Entrepreneurs typically work more hours and take fewer holidays than those at corporate jobs. A recent poll showed that 72% of entrepreneurs in the UK worked more than 50 hours, 59% worked more than 60 hours, and 32% put in more than 70 hours each week on their business. Holidays are few and far between: the same poll showed that 14% expected to be hard at work every single day for the next year. Only 53% would take even 2 weeks off.

One reason we entrepreneurs work so many hours is that there is no one telling us to go home or defining our work schedule. We

NEW WAYS OF DOING OLD THINGS / 87

make our own hours. Something that in theory sounds like the Life of Riley turns out to be the opposite. Each one of us is often the toughest boss we will ever have.

Being one's own boss manifests itself in many ways. You have to leave a Friday night party early because you are guiltily aware that you have to work in the morning. Another afternoon passes and you have again missed out on picking up your kids from school. Your friend is getting married and you can't go to the bachelor party in Vegas. The list goes on. Frustration mounts. Is this really how you want to live your life?

It doesn't have to be like this. There is another way.

Stever Robbins knows this way. Equipped with a Harvard MBA and a BS in computer science from MIT, he has played a key role in 9 start-ups, 5 IPOs, and 3 acquisitions. He has had more than his share of experience and knows which pitfalls to avoid. Stever explains one very helpful concept to entrepreneurs who can't seem to stop working and whose work days seem to be never ending:

'Decide in the morning what you will consider a full day's work TODAY. When you have done that, you can stop thinking about work. One of the reasons people find themselves preoccupied with their work even when they get home is that **they never stop and define for themselves what it means to have done a full day's work**. So they are always thinking – what else needs to be done overall, not what needs to be done TODAY?'

There is another very successful businessman who puts this principle into practice. N. R. Narayana Murthy is a self-made billionaire. The founder of Infosys, one of the largest IT services companies in India, he holds board positions on some of the most powerful companies, foundations and institutions in the world. He also holds 26 honorary doctorates.

Ranked as the 9th most admired CEO/chairman by the Economist Intelligence Unit – alongside Bill Gates, Steve Jobs and Warren Buffett – Murthy was also the most admired business leader in India for 5 years in a row. *Time* magazine placed him on the list of Asian heroes who had brought about revolutionary change and had the most significant impact on Asian history in the past 60 years, alongside Mahatma Gandhi, the Dalai Lama, Mother Teresa and Muhammad Ali.

Not unlike the Dalai Lama, Murthy is very grounded, calm and happy. You might think that someone with such enormous responsibility would have trouble living in the moment. Mr Murthy, however, does so with ease. When asked how he stays stress free after coming home from work and how he is able to focus completely on his home life, he shares his method:

'When we were much smaller, we would write a set of tasks to complete or make some progress on for that particular day. This is something I still do to this day, so when I leave the office, as long as I feel that I have given my best on those tasks and made progress, I am in a position to spend quality time with my family. When I come home with clear satisfaction that I have shown my passion and moved in the right direction, I have a sense of joy and inner peace. I have a sense of accomplishment, of self-worth. Therefore, when I see my family I can give them my full attention.'

So instead of trying to tackle your 'forever' list, purposefully make a 'today' list. Do the tasks. Feel good about it and then go pick up your kids, go on that trip or stay at that party as long you want. You've earned it.

ADJUSTMENT #2:
TURN YOUR TO DO LIST INTO A TODAY LIST

#3 KNOW SOMETHING ELSE

BY MARTIN BJERGEGAARD

Try visualising the news stream as seen from above. Imagine planet Earth with 7 billion people, more than 200 countries, and millions of tragedies and successes every day. Add a crop of journalists who've undertaken the task of finding the most interesting news, describing it as sensationally as possible and sharing it with the rest of us.

In addition, imagine all the knowledge that isn't news. All the science and insights on this planet. The educational system and the media industry that are constantly deciding which stories to communicate to the world. What the media chooses to cover is close to random. The field of possibility is so enormous that no one single person can have an overview. We all want to hear more about the cases we already know a little about, so once a story has been mentioned a few times, it becomes self-perpetuating. People are hungry for more.

The risk is that, **by following the regular news stream, you spend your time learning the same things as everyone else**. It gives you no real advantage, no special insights, nothing new to contribute to the world.

Picture your knowledge as a circle. Picture the knowledge of 'other people' as another circle. Your task is to create as little over-lap between the two circles as possible. Knowing something different from other people. This is where opportunities arise.

Christian Stadil, the owner of fashion company Hummel and a dozen other multimillion dollar enterprises, knew something about meditation, presence and Buddhism before most other business people in his industry, and this created a charisma and a brand that became pivotal to the empire he has since created. As a young man, Tony Hsieh, the co-founder and CEO of online retailer Zappos, experimented with giving his friends great party experiences and later used that quite rare (in business circles) knowledge to develop a unique culture at Zappos.

All *thought leaders* do it; they focus on developing new ideas, on discovering something that is not already common knowledge.

Several years ago while reading Tim Ferriss's international best-seller *The 4-Hour Workweek*, I made a decision and stopped following the news streams (thanks, Tim). This has resulted in a few funny situations, but no real problems. The interesting thing is that after a few months without news, a novel interest started growing in me; I wanted to acquire knowledge again, but knowledge in specific areas, which I had chosen myself, and was motivated to learn about.

By ditching your usual news channels and beginning the search for some new and rare insights, you can save time, while at the same time achieving more. It's also a lot more fun.

ADJUSTMENT #3:
BUILD YOUR OWN CIRCLE OF KNOWLEDGE

#4 PAUSE YOUR MIND

BY MARTIN BJERGEGAARD

Have you ever tried grappling with a complex problem that you simply could not find a solution for? You thought long and hard, used all of your brainpower and attempted to push yourself to come up with the answer. Then you gave up, went outside to mow the lawn, and bang – suddenly it was crystal clear to you.

What happened? You let your brain relax, and then, out of nowhere, it was ready to perform.

If you train with weights, you know that after 10 reps of bench-press, your muscles need a short break before they are ready for the next set. Runners know that interval training is the most effective type of exercise; first you run for a few minutes, hard and fast, then you take a few minutes' break.

The strange thing is that we haven't yet learned how to effectively use this obvious principle when it comes to the work of the brain. We still believe that we simply have to 'pull ourselves together', when our brain shows signs of fatigue. Of course, we do give the brain some breaks. At some point we shut down the computer, relax with a good movie, go to bed and sleep. The brain is charged for the following day and we go to work with the intent of thinking effectively for the next 8, 10 or 12 hours.

But the brain isn't designed for performing at its maximum level for hours on end. Just as with muscles, the optimal thing is to alternate between high activity and a relaxed pace at short intervals.

First, try thinking with focus and intensity for a while, then empty your head of all thoughts entirely and feel how 'present' you are in the moment – without assessing, analysing or judging. You're wide awake, but your head is completely empty. The breaks need only be a few seconds, and to others it is going to look as if you are in deep thought. But in reality you are doing the opposite. You are giving your brain a timeout, and when you let the thoughts back in, the solution will be obvious to you.

Eckhart Tolle, author of the international bestsellers *The Power of Now* and *A New Earth*, says: 'The simple reason why most scientists aren't creative is not that they don't know how to think, but that they don't know how to stop thinking.'

Intuitively, we all know that we need mental timeouts during the day, and we take them more or less unconsciously, like when we pick up a bottle of water or a cup of coffee, engage in small talk with a colleague or take a lunch break. But our breaks are too few, too random and too inefficient. Let's take a look:

Too few: to think optimally, you need closer to 50–100 breaks during the day than 5–10.

Too random: the break must be taken when your brain needs it, not when external circumstances such as the clock or colleagues demand it.

Too inefficient: most of us still think during our breaks, only it's usually about something other than the task we are dealing with. Maximum benefit can only be achieved if, during the break, we can stop thinking entirely.

Fatigue in the brain feels different from fatigue in the muscles. By learning to recognise the feeling, we can insert a few seconds' break exactly when we need it. By doing so we will enjoy clarity of thought many times every day, not only when we're mowing the lawn on Sundays.

ADJUSTMENT #4:
CONSCIOUSLY INSERT MIND-FREEING MOMENTS THROUGHOUT YOUR DAY

#5 FOCUS ON THE WILDLY IMPORTANT

BY MARTIN BJERGEGAARD

Our most loyal investor, Jannick B. Pedersen, owns the Scandinavian arm of FranklinCovey, the global training and consulting giant. The company was founded by Professor Stephen Covey, the icon behind many bestselling books on personal development and effectiveness, the most well-known of which is *The 7 Habits of Highly Effective People*.

When Jannick suggested that we buy one of his courses for our own company, we were quick to comply, though not because we are big fans of courses. Like most entrepreneurs, we're disciples of the 'learning by doing' philosophy. It was therefore with some trepidation that, 3 years ago, we closed down the company for two whole days and embarked on some joint training. To our surprise, however, these two days ended up being the most effective of all the thousands of days that we, combined, have worked at Rainmaking so far.

The theme of the course was 'Execution', and what we learned became a guiding principle both in Rainmaking and in all of our start-ups: Focusing on the Wildly Important.

From school we're accustomed to making a list of all the homework we have to do. When we go shopping, we write a shopping list of all the things we have to buy. In working life, the shopping

list is renamed a to-do list – and often made electronic. There are a myriad of systems to help you get the best overview of all your to-dos, including notifications at specific times and the ability to share items on your list with your colleagues. In just a short time, you and your team can generate a tremendous amount of tasks for yourselves and each other. You can even browse through them and follow their progress – if everybody remembers to update the system every time they do anything, that is.

That's all well and good, but there's an important insight that most of us overlook: at any given time there are 1–3 tasks in our business that are so important that, by comparison, everything else is a petty detail.

It can be closing an investment round so you avoid running out of money, taking care of a key employee who's about to quit, or focusing on making your product viral so that you get the scalable growth you dream about. Whatever it is, it is THAT task that is 'make it or break it'. The task that you and your team should be completely focused on.

But it's often easier to finish some smaller tasks on your to-do list rather than to try to tackle the big scary monster that is the Wildly Important. That's only human, and it's exactly why you need something else entirely (or at least something more) than extensive to-do lists: you need WIGS, WIGS boards and weekly WIGS sessions.

WIGS: Wildly Important Goals. Do you know what yours are? Find out with your team, and write them down in short and measurable sentences – for example, 'Our wildly important goal is to get our hit rate from 10% to 20% over the next 3 months.'

WIGS boards: You need a big whiteboard (or a screen) in the middle of the office, where you write the daily or weekly measurement of your WIGS, reminding everyone of it on a daily basis – for example, 'This week's hit rate: 12%.'

Weekly WIGS sessions: Meet up with the entire team once a week at a fixed time. Have the meeting last no more than 15 minutes. Everyone briefly shares what they have done since the last session to help you achieve your WIG – and says which single action they will do before the next session to get you even closer to the goal. (FranklinCovey has done research, and it turns out that if we try to reach more than 1–3 WIGS at a time, the probability of successful completion drops significantly.)

School has naturally influenced nearly all of us. We really want to be good. We want to produce a whole lot, and to be able to show off a list of tasks that we've already accomplished or are in the process of completing. It feels great to place that tick mark next to it when you've completed a task – or to delete a line on the long list. Many of us suffer from *tick mark mentality*.

It's easier to get ideas for tasks and add them on your to-do list than to be sharp, prioritise and cut some off. But that is the real challenge: FranklinCovey teaches us that the art of effective entrepreneurship and business management is to reduce, reduce, reduce – until you can zoom in on the few Wildly Important challenges.

A to-do list can still be an excellent idea. In his very useful book, *Getting Things Done*, David Allen explains how you can avoid stress by writing down all tasks in a secure system – thereby allowing your brain to let go of the idea. N. R. Narayana Murthy and Stever Robbins teach us how making a 'today' list can help define your work hours and set you free. Your Wildly Important task can also be written in there, and you can break it down into a number of sub-tasks, which together lead to the goal.

But the to-do list is a residual activity (i.e. something you work on when you need a break from the Wildly Important), not a place where you spend most of your working day. Start each morning by repeating to yourself what is Wildly Important – and visualise how you'll make a focused effort to get closer to your goal today.

By following this approach you'll find there are plenty of important (but not *wildly* important) tasks on your list that you never get to. But somehow, magically, you get maximum success anyway; and without having to wear yourself out, because you focus on the very few things that are 10, 100 or 1,000 times more important than everything else.

ADJUSTMENT #5:
DON'T TRY TO GET EVERYTHING DONE,
JUST THE FEW THINGS THAT REALLY MATTER

BEWARE THE TIME AND ENERGY WASTERS

→ 14 INSIGHTS TO HELP YOU NAVIGATE THE PITFALLS

It's amazing how much time and energy we all waste on a daily basis. It has been proven over and over again that 20% of our efforts bring in at least 80% of our results. The vast majority of our work doesn't add any significant value to either our success or our happiness.

The tricky part, of course, is to make the distinction between important tasks and time-wasting detours. The next 14 essays will provide you with guidance and inspiration towards that end. After reading them, identify your own elephant traps: the huge time-wasting holes that you fall into on a regular basis.

The things that burn daylight will be different for all of us.

For some it may be unnecessary conflicts, for others being inefficient about raising money, and for others still it may be delaying difficult decisions.

Take a moment to identify what your particular elephant traps are and then work to systematically address them. Start by getting the fundamentals right. Of course, you can find an abundance of advice about efficiency. But what you need more than anything else are some basic building blocks. Here they are.

'It has been my observation that most people get ahead during the time that others waste' – Henry Ford

#1 KNOW WHEN TO PULL THE PLUG

BY JORDAN MILNE

We all know someone who has been working on getting their venture going for as long as we've known them. In fact, that person may very well have been us at some point in time. Whether the trouble is with assembling a team, building the product, establishing partnerships or getting traction, the idea just doesn't seem to be taking off.

One of the biggest wastes of time is working on a project that has no legs. It affects our balance and happiness, as we work too hard without reaping the rewards of our efforts.

On the flipside most of us have also heard stories of entrepreneurs who have achieved their success through great persistence and tenacity after hustling for many years, and it seems obvious to credit their success to their perseverance.

So what should we do? How do we navigate the paradox of when to persevere and when to call it a day? When to fish or when to cut bait?

Brad Feld and David Cohen are co-founders of TechStars, one of the most successful start-up accelerators in the world. TechStars operates programmes in Boulder, Boston, Seattle and New York City.

Through mentorship and seed funding they help young companies grow. More than 70% of their participating start-ups succeed in closing an investor deal for hundreds of thousands or even millions of dollars right after the 3-month programme.

Very few people have seen more start-ups than Brad and David. Drawing from their wealth of experience they shared their thoughts on the paradox with us to help you decide when you should push on and when you should cut your losses.

David says that you ought to consider quitting if:

- you can't stop thinking about what else you might be doing with your time or resources instead;
- that 'other thing' keeps calling you;
- you've lost your passion and are constantly distracted.

Or you are about to make your fourth or fifth major pivot (meaning that your concept has changed drastically many times since conception – an iterative process is healthy, but it also has limits).

'Ups and downs are only natural. When you feel that you want to quit, wait 48 hours. Maybe take a few days off. If you still feel that way, consider really quitting. If not, there is nothing to worry about,' David explains. He also proposes a visualisation exercise. Take a day to visualise one outcome: stopping your current project, and starting a new one. Identify yourself with that decision. How does it make you feel? What mood does it put you in?

The next day, completely change your mindset: visualise being committed to your current project and coming into the office for the next few years and working to overcome the challenges and build your company. And then ask yourself, which of these two scenarios excites you the most?

David states that on a non-personal level, quitting should come from being intellectually honest. What is the market really telling you?

For most of us the term 'quitting' has a negative connotation, unjustifiably so. One of the reasons many entrepreneurs persist is indeed because of this stigma. They don't want to 'give up'. Stopping a venture, however, is in many circumstances not bad. Often it's the right thing to do and will lead to your next opportunity, the one that will afford you success, balance and happiness. A better term for quitting is to seek out a 'new opportunity platform'.

Continuously evaluate both your ventures and your mindset in relation to them. Make the tough decisions, and when you do, Cohen says, 'Realise that you will never know for sure that you are making the right decision. Entrepreneurs make decisions in the absence of 100% of the data all the time. This is no different.'

Most importantly, realise that failure can be a very important part of the process. Listen to the wisdom in the saying 'there is no such thing as failure, only feedback'. In other circumstances those same actions could have had a different outcome. Learn from the failure, and get back out there.

When you are faced with a difficult decision it is hard to keep things in perspective. Three tough months looks much harder looking forward than looking back. If you need to do something difficult and feel the urge to put it off: don't. Start that clock ticking now. You can either get on your way to putting it behind you or have it linger over your head. As I tell myself when I go to the dentist … no matter what happens, in 30 minutes I will be out of that chair.

Often when things start to fail we get a false sense of urgency that we need to make it work no matter what. When we are locked into something and it fails we can lose sight of opportunities. We need to remember that those who succeed see opportunities everywhere.

Try to acknowledge that sometimes your past experiences may have a sunk cost. Don't fall into the casino trap of continuing to 'up your bet'. Instead, adopt the mindset that you are just starting your business today with everything you know now. Unplug and reset. Today honestly is the first day of the rest of your life. What will you choose to do?

TIME SAVER #1:
CHOOSE THE RIGHT PROJECT

#2 DON'T 'MAKE IT WORK'

BY MARTIN BJERGEGAARD

Years ago when I worked as a management consultant at McKinsey & Co., I heard an expression which, at the time, I didn't think too much about. The partner would ask his project manager about a person within the client company and whether he was collaborative and good to work with. The project manager would nod slightly, the air thick with reservations, and I would hear him say: 'I can make it work.' This was McKinsey code and meant that the relationship was tense, but the consultant, through empathy and influence techniques, would turn the collaboration into a success, whatever the cost.

Meet Ole Høyer. Adviser to top executives on how to optimise their energy and performance, and a man who takes a different approach.

'I believe that we humans are vibrating at different energy frequencies – and when we meet someone on the same frequency, that's when we get in flow and can co-create and accomplish great results without pain or sacrifice,' Ole says. We all recognise it in ourselves. Working together with some people, we can go on at full power for hours on end and it feels like playing. With others, a single meeting feels like an eternity and we're drained of energy when the session is finally over. Call it chemistry, connection or mutual understanding. These are the people we look forward to seeing, and those who help make us capable of accomplishing more than we had ever dreamed of by ourselves.

But too often we settle for less. We meet a person who has something we want and even though our internal warning bells sound, we swallow the discomfort, and enter the relationship to reach the desired outcome. Most of us have a customer, colleague, business partner or investor who fits that description. Ole reminds us that it's not only a bad idea from a happiness perspective, but also a waste of good energy which in turn leads to lower overall performance.

'I emit a certain energy and some clients get attracted to this, and others don't. To provide my product I require close cooperation with the client, and I don't try to persuade anyone who isn't ready for my message. Instead, I follow the energy where it goes and as a result I have very few client meetings that don't result in collaboration,' he says.

His product is just as important as it is unusual; training executives in optimising their energy and fulfilling their purpose in life. Ole and his team of coaches run in intervals, meditate, do eye-contact exercises, and discuss emotional stability and spiritual awareness with their participants. Although all this may sound a little 'new age' the customer list certainly isn't:

Goldman Sachs, Deloitte, Novartis, Scandinavia's biggest bank, Nordea, and the large Swiss bank UBS are among their most loyal customers.

Ole is successful and relaxed at the same time. He started being self-employed just before the financial crisis, and while thousands of other small consulting firms have succumbed, he has experienced constant growth. He spends 20% of his time providing his product and the other 80% on travelling, developing himself further, and preparing to be at peak performance during his courses.

He has started his own charity in India that runs schools and facilitates microloans for the rural population. He travels to meditation and yoga retreats in the Bahamas, in Switzerland overlooking the mountains, and by the beaches of southern India, and he loves to dance 5Rhythms for hours on his many trips to New York.

The secret? 'I have no special prerequisites to do what I do. I'm just a banker who one day got tired of suits and numbers. I spent a couple of years on finding my purpose in life, and optimising my own energy. Now, I inspire others to do the same. If there is a secret, it's that I dare to follow my energy. Most people expect that the energy continues to be there, even when they walk away from it,' Ole shares.

If you want to be energetic, then make sure to engage in activities that excite you, and to be together with people who recharge

and inspire you. When you compromise on the energy, a short-term gain often turns into a long-term nuisance. Be true to your energy and feel where it draws you.

TIME SAVER #2:
AVOID PEOPLE WHO DRAIN YOUR ENERGY

#3 GAIN YOUR EXTRA MONTH

BY JORDAN MILNE

What would you do with one extra month? An entire 30 days that's all yours. Perhaps you would use the time to further your business by focusing more on marketing or by studying with an expert in your field. Or maybe you'd take a little adventure: explore the far corners of the earth, raft down the Colorado River or hang glide in Brazil. Or maybe you'd choose something altogether different, like planting your herb garden or learning to play the piano.

Now what if I told you that this free month is not just a one-off, but that you get one every single year? Furthermore, what if you already have this time off but you just don't realise it yet? And what are many of us currently doing with these precious hours? It must be something terribly important, right, to justify so much time? It turns out, however, that with this precious month of our lives we are simply sitting in our cars. That's right. Sitting in our cars.

The cover of the 17 January 2011 issue of *Macleans*, Canada's national magazine, revealed a startling truth: 'Canadians spend the equivalent of 32 working days a year stuck in traffic'.

Even if you're a Canadian who enjoys playing music in your car, learning Italian or listening to Harry Potter on tape you would

be hard pressed to find one person who thinks this is a good use of that much time. When compared to other ways of spending a month, how often do you think sitting in traffic would crack the top 10 or even the top 100?

For Canadians who commute, the cumulative time spent in traffic is overwhelming. If you work from the ages of 25 to 65 that adds up to 3.75 years spent driving to and from work. For many there will be an additional ripple of negatives as the pressure to make up for lost time forces us to work on our mobile phones whilst driving in heavy traffic, which is both stressful and dangerous.

But maybe this problem is unique to those crazy Canadians? Their ice roads and dog sleds must be at fault? Not so. The time and energy spent on commuting is indeed a global phenomenon. In Germany a study showed that people with long journeys to and from work are systematically worse off and report significantly lower life satisfaction. While it sounds shockingly high, 32 days a year translates into little more than 2 hours of commuting per day – not an outrageous stretch in itself.

A study of commuters in Dublin, Ireland, revealed that nearly 80% found travelling to work to be a stressful experience. That's something very stressful to do twice a day. Regular commuters who work in city centres often opt for larger houses far from the city instead of choosing a smaller home closer to their office. In doing so they often overestimate the happiness that the added square footage will bring them compared to the 2 hours they will lose every day commuting to and from work.

It's true that sometimes commuting is really the only option, but, given the cost, we should set out to reduce it by all means possible. **We can lessen the blow by using strategies such as working from home, even if it's just for one day a week.**

Perhaps better yet, run or bike to work. Most of us agree with the benefits of exercise. The challenge is to find the time, and this is where entrepreneur and chef Claus Meyer has found a veritable treasure trove of extra time.

'Most of us spend several hours a week in transit in one form or another. Every time I go from A to B, I've made it a habit to ask myself: can I walk, run or cycle the distance instead of taking a taxi, car or train?

'There's always an "opportunity cost" to exercise. When I enter the badminton court, I simultaneously step away from something else. The challenge is that this "other thing" should be as unimportant as possible. I never play sports in the evening, because I want to spend that time with my family. But an 8-km trip across Copenhagen doesn't take me much longer to run than to drive. If my colleague doesn't want to run along, he can bring me clean clothes, I can take it in a backpack, or I can send it in advance with a taxi. A workout is worth much more than $40 to me.' In this way Claus cheats the clock every day, and steals an hour from nothingness.

'Some may think it's a bit strange to arrive sweaty and in need of a shower before a meeting, but most people just smile and to me it's a roar of freedom. When I run around in the middle of the city while people are stuck in their cars, I get a kick that goes beyond what the run itself gives me. I feel free and privileged,' Claus says.

Even in transit this approach can be powerful. The prospect of a 5-hour wait at the airport in Bangkok combined with Claus's attitude towards exercise drove him to seek out an opportunity most of us might have overlooked. Through contacts in the Danish Badminton Federation, he lined up a training session with a top player in the Royal Badminton Club in Bangkok.

Forty minutes after leaving the airport he stood face to face with the player ranked 35th in Thailand. This resulted in a good run into every corner of the court, a pounding pulse in the humid heat and a memory for life.

Two hours later Claus was back at the airport, his body feeling great, freshly washed, deeply grateful, a few hundred per cent more content than most other people waiting for their flight, and ready to look after his daughters while his wife got a well-deserved massage.

TIME SAVER #3:
IF YOU HAVE TO GET FROM A TO B,
BE SMART ABOUT IT

#4 DON'T SEND THAT EMAIL

BY MARTIN BJERGEGAARD

There was a time when letters were something that you wrote by hand or typewriter, and put on the table or in a drop box (a physical one) to be posted the next day. Obviously, this was a slow process, but it had the advantage of giving you the chance to change your mind. I wonder how many letters over the years have been torn to pieces before reaching their intended destination, because the author regained composure fast enough to find a better form of expression.

In that respect email is lethal: if your emotions have taken over, nothing is more satisfying than to dash off your anger in the safe confines of your email program. Something psychological happens when you write an email to a person you're angry with or suspicious about. Most of us have experienced this: a growing sense of our own certainty and self-righteousness. A pulsing negativity that grows as we write, climaxing in a feeling of certainty that now – with this well-expressed message – we are finally setting the record straight, and that this will now force them to realise how unfairly they've behaved. One click and, without a chance to change one's mind, the mail hits the recipient in the face like a clenched fist.

What seemed effective in the heat of the moment suddenly

escalates. Maybe our recipient fires off an even hotter response. Or maybe they know better and suggest meeting face to face in order to clear the air.

No matter what, our hot-headed mail has cost us dearly in our efficiency account; now we have to talk things through, confidence needs to be rebuilt, and new agreements have to be made.

What could have been done in 10 minutes (had we had the foresight to pick up the phone, ask our questions and sincerely listen to the answer) has now become an unwelcome and energy-draining task that can easily add up to several hours and even more bad karma.

Email has triumphed as a form of communication because it's a very effective way to communicate a wide variety of messages; a meeting date, a note, considerations before a strategy meeting. But when emotions are involved, email is among the worst tools for communication. What's written is so easily misunderstood. We often misinterpret the tone of an email, and it can often create more distance than it bridges.

The person I know who is best at avoiding this pitfall is my partner and colleague in Rainmaking, Morten Kristensen. We have been friends since we were 15 years old, and business partners for almost a decade. During that time, Morten has managed to NEVER send me an emotional email, a feat I cannot claim to have fully matched. I asked Morten to write down his miracle recipe and here it is:

A) Write the email and think carefully about what you believe to be fair and unfair – try to put yourself in the recipient's place. Might his or her experience of the facts be different from yours?

B) When you've written the email, do not send it. Instead, do the following:

1) Think about whether it's possible to meet with the recipient face to face instead and talk about it. If so, then do it.

2) If a face-to-face meeting is not possible, then read through your email again and remove any text which has no forward-looking purpose, but is only meant to provoke or to make yourself feel better.

3) Get someone else to read the mail and comment on it honestly – and get that person to put himself in the recipient's shoes.

C) If, despite your attempts at toning down your communication, you get an angry email in return, then refrain from participating in escalating the conflict. Now is the time to calm things down again – and that's your responsibility. Get the person on the phone or meet them face to face.

Make a habit of never writing emails when you're angry, disappointed or suspicious. And never bring up emotional issues with the computer as a middleman. Otherwise, a single email can easily turn into half a day's extra work.

TIME SAVER #4:
DEAL WITH CONFLICTS IN PERSON

#5 BE DECISIVE WHEN IT COUNTS

BY MARTIN BJERGEGAARD

It was the first annual meeting with our bank adviser. He was impressed with our results and the growth we had achieved in Rainmaking. 'But,' he said, 'the true measure of strength will be if you can also downsize when needed and make the really difficult decisions.'

Entrepreneurs are typically good at coming up with ideas, expanding and developing. We are, however, less experienced and slower on the trigger when it comes to laying off team members, turning down new customers and opportunities and wrapping up failed ventures.

What gives an entrepreneur longevity is his or her ability to make unpopular and difficult, yet necessary, decisions and implement them quickly and consistently.

Often when we get lucky and hit the jackpot with a project we feel like we can walk on water. **But without the ability to make tough decisions and carry them out without hesitation, our success will sooner or later come to an end**.

We didn't disappoint our bank adviser. At the following annual meeting we were able to tell him that we had closed three of our homegrown start-ups and said goodbye to 10 of our team members since saw him the previous year. Doing so was extremely difficult and we didn't take the decisions lightly. It had required all of our empathy and strength to implement them in a way that enabled everyone to move on positively. We knew deep down that, although difficult, these actions were the right thing to do.

It can take many years for a large, well-oiled business to implement changes that are necessary. For example, it took several years in the red before the Danish toy giant LEGO started outsourcing its production, selling amusement parks and liquidating failing areas of its business. In a start-up it is necessary to make such decisions much faster.

Firing a CEO is one of the most unpleasant business experiences many of us can imagine. A lay-off can cause mental scars for years to come. Add to that the fact that when you lay off a CEO it is commonplace to ask them to leave the office the very same day. If they stick around, their disappointment and frustration will suck the energy out of the whole team, and a feeling of uncertainty about the future of the company will prevent everyone from both feeling good and getting work done. You need to contain the negative energy and reinstate certainty immediately.

This experience became a reality for me a few years ago. One of our companies was doing very well and we hired a CEO from outside the firm to take it to the next level. He was solid, likeable and had an impressive background. He was also a bit older than us and we were proud of the fact that he wanted to work with us.

What started off with great promise quickly went south. After 6 months I got the sense that something was wrong. I had my hands full with a new start-up, but had been keeping up to date through regular reviews of the Key Performance Indicators. The growth rate was very strong, but when you took a closer look at the numbers it turned out that we were losing 10% of our customers every month. It was only because of a heavy inflow of new customers that we were still growing.

In this specific industry, such a big customer turnover is completely unacceptable. When I delved further into the cause it turned out that customers were leaving due to a high percentage of severely delayed deliveries. Immediately I dropped everything and started working with the CEO on an action plan. After two weeks it became clear that his profile was not right for the job at hand. He was just not the right person.

This was hard for me to stomach as hiring him had been mainly my decision. I had misjudged the situation. It was clear what had to be done and there was no time to waste. Fourteen days later I invited the CEO for a meeting. Just one hour later, after giving him the news that he had to be let go, I presented a new CEO to the rest of the team.

When you're in a situation where someone isn't up to the task, more often than not that person is not only aware of it but also not enjoying the situation either. It is usually best for both parties to go their separate ways. Even if they have come to feel comfortable in the position they would probably feel more fulfilled somewhere else where they are a better fit.

We have experienced our fair share of failures in Rainmaking. The wrong strategies, the wrong people and too many new projects in too short a period of time. The main reason we are still going strong is that we have been good at making hard decisions, here and now.

TIME SAVER #5:
DON'T DELAY TOUGH DECISIONS

#6 STREAMLINE YOUR LIFE

BY MARTIN BJERGEGAARD

If you have ever sipped a cold Budweiser on a hot summer's day then you owe just a little something to a town called Leuven. Leuven is the capital of the province of Flemish Brabant in Belgium. It is the birthplace of Anheuser-Busch InBev, the single largest brewing company on earth. It is also the birthplace of Sophie Vandebroek. Raised in Belgium, Sophie went on to earn a Master's degree in electro-mechanical engineering from Katholieke Universiteit and later a PhD in electrical engineering from the Ivy League university Cornell.

Sophie is a self-proclaimed 'intrapreneur', meaning that she is an entrepreneur within a large corporation, XEROX.

Like most entrepreneurs she enjoys the challenge of coming up with new and exciting products, but unlike most entrepreneurs she also has the responsibility of managing a large team and working within the sometimes bureaucratic infrastructure of a major corporation.

'We always come up with ideas that we hope will make a big impact on our customers. Many of those, however, will also disrupt the status quo within the company and within our current technologies and product lines. In order to be an "intrapreneur" you need to have confidence because there will be lots of barriers in getting the "ship" to move in the direction you want it to. You have to make sure that all your team members and management, as well as the total value-chain to bring the idea to the market, buy into your concepts. And in my experience, to be able to genuinely influence others you have to feel good yourself. You cannot feel like that unless you have achieved your balance,' Sophie says.

She herself had this balance, lost it following the death of her husband, and has since regained it.

When she suddenly became a single mother with three small children, many people told her the only way to cope would be to pull back on her career. She knew, however, that the best chance of long-term happiness for her and her family would only come if she kept the job she was so passionate about. Instead, to regain her balance Sophie began developing a new set of strategies. One of them was to streamline both her personal and professional life.

'What I realised was that there are so many things that we either worry about or do that are just completely unimportant. They are not going to make you happy or help you achieve balance. They are also not going to help determine your performance at work or whether your company or the project is going to be successful. And so I looked and said – what can I stop doing?' Sophie tells us.

In her personal life Sophie hired a student once a week to do the grocery shopping. The extra cost, she says, was easily outweighed by fewer impulse purchases. She sold her husband's boat so that she wouldn't need to take care of it. She found a new format for holidays that turned out to be not only less stressful to plan but also more fun for her children, namely camping. Sophie also decided to forego organising social events, which freed up lots of her evening and weekend time, and didn't really hurt anyone as others took over where she left off. Next, she did something many would consider unthinkable: streamlining her relationships to focus fully on a handful of close friends, prioritising the quality of those important relationships over sheer quantity.

In her business life she took a similar approach. She cut down on paperwork, such as writing reports and newsletters that were often not read. With the help of the lean-minded 'six sigma' method she simplified many of her internal processes and made a motivated effort to increase empowerment in every corner of her organisation.

So, using Sophie Vandebroek as your inspiration, **take a look into your own life, at all of the activities and tasks that make up your day. Do they all contribute to the advancement of your business, or make you or those you care about happy?** If not, what can you cut out?

Personally, I found some nice pockets of wasted time that I could eliminate when I did the exercise a couple of years ago: I no longer spend any time driving to work, cleaning or gardening, reading newspapers, or even ironing shirts or dressing up in fancy suits. Why not? Because I found out that those activities added little if anything to either my happiness or my performance. And I think it is pretty unlikely that I will some day regret that I did not spend more time vacuum cleaning.

Of course, it took a couple of conscious decisions to cut out doing what I didn't want to do. I live just over 2 miles from our office, so it only takes me 10 minutes to bike there every day. I have chosen to live in a flat, so there is no garden work and very little home maintenance. And I dress more like the entrepreneurs of Silicon Valley than the investment bankers of London. We each have our own set of priorities, but too often we don't live according to them. That leaves us a great opportunity to improve both our happiness and our performance by once in a while streamlining our lives.

TIME SAVER #6:
CLEAR YOUR AGENDA OF ACTIVITIES THAT DON'T ADD VALUE TO YOUR LIFE

#7 USE YOUR PERISCOPE

BY JORDAN MILNE

Your business is your life. It's all you can think about. You wake up with it on your mind and lie restless in bed at night with it still in your thoughts. You're starting to get tunnel vision.

While focus is important, there is a difference between putting energy into the task at hand and getting so caught up that you forget to look at the bigger picture.

Caterina Fake, co-founder of Flick'r, explains: 'You can get too involved in your company and miss opportunities both outside of work as well as for your business. By keeping your head buried in "work", not only do you miss out on great moments as they happen, but you're also hurting your chances at success.'

When you are immersed in work it is like being in a submarine. Just as a submarine uses a periscope to assess conditions outside its immediate environment and confirm targets and threats, so too can the manager of a business. Open your eyes and use your periscope more often.

When you're in the thick of it, remember that having a look around is part of focusing. It might seem like you're taking your eye off the ball, but it is in fact the opposite. Taking a step back enables you to see the big picture.

'Business is a dynamic game. Those that adapt prevail. To adapt you need to see what's coming and react. To be able to see what's coming you need to pop your head up once in a while, take a deep breath and see what's going on outside of your frantic bubble,' Caterina says.

Tunnel vision can manifest itself in many ways. Tech companies are often guilty of focusing on product features at the expense of understanding their customers. Teams execute their strategy only to find that the market has changed.

What is it about coming back from a good holiday that has you focusing on the right stuff and being more efficient? After taking time away, you often get a fresh perspective, returning to work with a clearer view of what is important. Have you ever tried coming back from holiday and without hesitation eliminating a handful of tasks on your to-do list; or found yourself with that groundbreaking new insight that could take your start-up to the next level? Why can this only happen twice a year: over the Christmas holiday and on the summer break? Why can't this happen every month or week, or even every day?

Try changing your physical environment or get in motion. Take a weekend getaway or go somewhere you've never been before and you will find yourself at peak performance on Monday morning. These are all ways of 'putting up your periscope' and sneaking a look outside your bubble, whether it is for 5 minutes or 5 months.

TIME SAVER #7:
DON'T LET THE DETAILS KEEP YOU
FROM SEEING THE BIG PICTURE

#8 KEEP AWAY FROM PREDATORS

BY MARTIN BJERGEGAARD

In business as in nature, predators are a fact of life. Some people want to take advantage of us and deceive us. They can be charismatic, cunning and hard to spot: the seemingly helpful venture capitalist who, from behind the scenes, manipulates a cash-strapped entrepreneur so he can insist on a majority share; the partner who deploys the numbers to pay us less than we are entitled to.

Luckily, as the days go by, the predators become fewer and further between, unable to survive in a transparent world. Despite this, predators are a fact of life and we have to deal with them even though it seems a waste of our valuable energy.

The most effective attitude we can have is to enter each new relationship with trust and an open mind. Nine out of ten people will reciprocate this kind of behaviour, and that is far more valuable than what happens that tenth time when we stumble upon a cheat. In nature, encountering a predator can be fatal. In business, we won't lose our lives, but it can still result in tragedy. With awareness, however, we can avert predators, steer clear of their dangers and focus on all of our positive relationships.

To achieve more in life and for your businesses to succeed, it is important that you never make the same mistakes twice. Learn the lesson when you uncover a predator. Get away quickly and never go back. Do not waste any more time or energy on it. Return to your trusting mode and find new peers who encourage and reward your positive attitude. You don't have to cooperate with everyone; it is perfectly all right to pick out the ones who give you energy and happiness and to back off from those who seek to exhaust or use you, whether they do this consciously or not.

Dealing with 'assholes' is such a huge waste of time. Don't put up with it, and just as importantly: don't let it turn you into one yourself.

TIME SAVER #8:
DON'T DEAL WITH, OR BE, AN ASSHOLE

#9 RELEASE YOUR GRIP

BY JORDAN MILNE

We are in the middle of doing something we love. Maybe it's playing with our kids or eating out with our friends. Everyone seems focused on what is in front of them, enjoying each others' company, chatting and laughing ... but we are having trouble staying in the moment. Our mind keeps wandering back to what's going on in our business. Is everything getting done? Are we working on the right things? Should we be working now?

It's a terrible feeling, but we can't help it. Our family and friends seem to notice that we are not 'all there' and we become painfully aware that we are missing a valuable moment. And yet, we can't seem to help ourselves. **There is no point being away from work if your mind never leaves the office**. What's more, sitting there fretting about it isn't going to accomplish anything.

'Worrying is like a rocking chair – it gives you something to do, but it gets you nowhere' – Glen Turner

Living this way leads to regret and is in essence the worst of both worlds. A far cry from the goal of enjoying your time away from work AND building a great business. Mitch Thrower, serial entrepreneur and Ironman triathlete, shares with us one of the most important disciplines that helps him to live in the moment and to stay stress free away from work:

'Surround yourself with people who you trust and who you can let make mistakes and release control to. Entrepreneurs are by definition control freaks. This is one thing that gets us into trouble from a work/life balance perspective. The trick is to make sure things are done well, not necessarily in the exact way you had envisioned it. You need to make a clear distinction between something getting done and something getting done your way.'

By trusting those you work with to get the job done, you free up a large space in your mind. What's more, by sharing control you may be pleasantly surprised by the unexpected directions your venture takes as a result of this new input.

TIME SAVER #9:
RELAX AND LET OTHERS CONTRIBUTE

#10 MAKE YOUR BUSINESS PLAN LIGHT AND AGILE

BY MARTIN BJERGEGAARD

In business schools and universities all over the world students are taught to make business plans. These plans are a specific and analytical way of relating to a new business idea. How big is the market? Who is the competition? How will the turnover develop from year to year? Five-year budgets and detailed projections. While there may be some merit to this as an academic exercise, it has become far too much of a focus for many entrepreneurs. The reality is that it is all guesswork. A case of academic imagination.

In his bestselling book *REWORK*, Jason Fried of 37 Signals puts it succinctly: 'Estimates that stretch weeks, months and years into the future are fantasies.' We couldn't agree more. And we are not alone.

Peer Kølendorf is a Danish serial entrepreneur with 5 exits under his belt, the biggest of which brought in $30 million, as well as being an associate professor at INSEAD. He always begins his lessons by reminding the students that whatever they put in their business plan, it will probably not hold up.

'Then they look all perplexed and start searching for errors in the spreadsheets,' says Peer in his cheerful manner.

It's not the students' fault. **It's just simply arrogant to believe you can predict how a start-up will perform 5 years into the future**. To spend a lot of your precious time formulating guesses is a waste of effort.

Millions of hours are wasted every year as bright people toil away over PowerPoints and business plans that will never come to fruition. Most businesses are iterative and change over time. The point when most people are writing their plan is the time when they are the least equipped to do so. Thinking that you know and can control everything is also a dangerous frame of mind to start with when launching a business. Acknowledge that you have a lot to learn and let the customers' actions direct you.

If you need to convince potential investors or the bank, you probably have to bite the bullet and write a fable about your start-up (more about that soon). Luckily, investors are starting to come to their senses; many of them no longer have the appetite to chew through 50 pages of PowerPoint presentations and endless fictitious projections. They too have started experimenting with new ways of evaluating a start-up, for instance by following its progress for a while before investing, or even coming along to customer meetings.

Business plans are usually fostered and embraced in the college system because they are something concrete that can be easily evaluated by a teacher. They are then perpetuated elsewhere, as we often take our cues from educational institutions.

It's alarming to think that you can spend 4–6 years at college studying business and still not emerge with some of the most current and important skills needed to get your business off the ground. It's true that you can learn valuable skills such as cold calling, designing mock-ups, making viral videos and building Facebook pages elsewhere, but why not use your time at college to learn something that makes a real difference?

Accelerator programmes like Techstars, Y Combinator and Startupbootcamp have achieved great success. They certainly don't ask to see (never mind read) business plans as part of their application process. Instead you fill out a form with fewer than 20 questions. If you pass that first hurdle, the next step is a 10-minute phone conversation, followed by a longer phone conversation and finally, if you are still in the running, a meeting in person.

If you are reading this book, in all likelihood you have heard of a company called Groupon, *the fastest growing company of all time*. Surely such a success must have been planned from day one? Not so. Groupon was actually started as a side project of a collective action venture called The Point, and it just so happened that it took off. As we have said, business is an iterative process. The vast majority of start-ups change their course constantly based on market feedback until they find something that sticks.

Instead of wasting your time on a business plan, it is better to write a simple one-pager outlining the vision, the values, a few key numbers and the three most important immediate actions of your proposed venture – and then get started on some real work.

Call up customers, build your product, get some press interest or adjust your Adwords campaign. And when you are finished, you can go home without feeling bad about not having a full 5-year business plan.

TIME SAVER #10:
GET TO THE POINT

#11 STOP HIDING OUT

BY MARTIN BJERGEGAARD

He had a likeable approach and radiated good energy. The room was filled with 50–60 software developers and entrepreneurs, and he had 3 minutes and 3 slides to present his idea, generate interest and try to get some co-founders on board.

He started off: 'I have a great idea to make a portal for scuba diving. I am a schoolteacher and have not been involved in entrepreneurship before. I need some co-founders, in particular a good programmer.' Then there were a few pictures of scuba diving and diving equipment. That was the whole pitch.

A programmer in the front row with a laptop on his knees raised his hand and asked a question: 'Can you tell us more about your idea?' The answer from the up and coming entrepreneur was polite but firm: 'I would rather not at this time.'

He continued in as friendly a manner as possible: 'I am afraid to say too much because it is a really good idea and someone might steal it.' Then the dialogue ended, the audience applauded reservedly and the schoolteacher sat back down on his chair.

This is a true story and unfortunately not the only one of its kind I have experienced.

At Rainmaking people often ask us: 'How do you keep your ideas secret?' I now have an answer, but the first few times I was asked this I got caught off guard because I simply did not understand their logic at all. We put a great amount of thought into the best ways we can spread the word about our ideas. Why in the world would we keep them secret? Do you know anyone who has been successful with a secret idea?

Our first view of the world is through our own eyes. This is natural. If we don't evolve past this, however, we will often mistakenly see ourselves as the centre of the universe. Yes, we are our own centre, but others have their own lives, agendas and dreams. To believe that people you meet are just sitting around waiting to steal your idea borders on delusions of grandeur.

The founders of Skype passed the hat around for a long time before they found anyone willing to invest in their project. Today we think their idea was genius and that we just might have stolen it if we had heard about it in time, but most likely, back in 2003, we would have listened politely to Janus Friis and Niklas Zennström and then continued on with what we were already doing. We would have gone on to create what we, ourselves, were passionate about.

The nature of motivation and human mentality does not work so simply as to effortlessly exchange our own projects and ideas for those of others.

In any case it is highly unlikely that, after hearing Janus and Niklas's pitch, you would have been able to create Skype – even if you had wanted to. Having an idea is said to represent somewhere between 1 and 5% of the necessary ingredients for a successful company. The remaining 95–99% comes down to execution. Successful execution requires the coordination of many elements that can't be acquired quickly, including the right competences and network.

There is a lot to be gained by telling people about your idea. You receive valuable input and reactions, which help to develop your idea further. You might even build great contacts with potential customers, experts and investors. The more you talk about your idea the better it becomes, the more others can help you and the more committed you become to your project. **An idea that only exists in your head will quickly fade away from lack of nurturing**.

Relationships are one of the most important assets for an entrepreneur and are created by showing trust and interacting with other people. If you refuse to tell others about your ideas you unwillingly send a signal that you don't have much faith in their morals and their ability to come up with ideas of their own.

Don't waste valuable time by hiding out in stealth mode. Take a cold turkey approach by writing a detailed blog post on your current best idea. Tell everyone you meet about it. Have confidence and see what happens.

TIME SAVER #11:

TAKE EVERY OPPORTUNITY TO GET PEOPLE
EXCITED ABOUT YOUR PROJECT

#12 KNOW HOW TO RAISE MONEY

BY MARTIN BJERGEGAARD

You have decided your start-up needs a round of external capital to develop as fast and efficiently as possible. Probably a worthy decision, but also the first step on a path that can lead to frightening inefficiency.

How many times have you tried to complete an investment round? Once, twice or maybe even three times? For most entrepreneurs raising capital is a rare event.

Fortunately, once we've got the money, we'll usually spend some time focusing on running and developing the company before we need to go at it again.

But that also means that very few entrepreneurs feel truly comfortable with the task. Not least because the investment climate changes faster than fashion in Paris.

One year investors want to see aggressive growth plans, the next year it's solid earnings forecasts. Some moneymen mostly focus on the team, others on the vision. European investors will consider opportunities for a long time, Americans make quick decisions, and the Japanese want to drink you under the table. It's a jungle, and as an entrepreneur, you are more often the intimidated prey than the lion king.

PLAN
BOSS
YES
NO
TOP
M.
32x
x 20
$100000
MORE?
ONE YEAR
TWISE OR ?
$1000000 (NEED MORE $!)
TOTAL $4 000 000 ? + 200 000
ECONOMY
$100000

The result can easily be that you drift around unfocused. You have to keep your business running with one hand, while raising money with the other. You have tons of meetings, but none of them really yield results, or you have a hard time getting any investors to talk at all.

Gradually, the process develops into something that is far from the well of abundance you had hoped for; and while the bank account isn't receiving the reinforcements it needs, you also lose momentum in your business – a lethal combination.

At Rainmaking, we've raised $10 million over 5 years, spread out across 10 of our start-ups (the rest we've funded internally), and we've been through both beautiful and tedious processes. Along the road we've optimised our approach and have arrived at 7 insights:

1) Expect it to take **6 months** from when you start the process until the money is in the account. If things go faster (and they rarely do), then you have good news instead of a bankruptcy. And raise money for at least 12 months, preferably 18 months, so that you and your organisation will have a period of undisturbed work before potentially having to think about fundraising again.

2) **Dedicate one of the founders** (the best salesman) full-time to fundraising throughout the entire process. Raising capital should not be a residual task, nor can it be delegated. During fundraising you need to show continued

traction, so split up the workload and 'protect' the rest of the team from being distracted by the investors and all of their questions.

3) **Make state-of-the-art material** before having your first meeting. Most investors still want to be impressed with documents, so without the glitter you'll always be one step behind and won't be taken seriously. Sad but true.

4) **Understand the finances** of your project. Financial operations are usually very simple in a start-up, but it's crucial that you understand what drives your revenue and your variable costs, and how these numbers evolve as you grow. Benchmark against competitors or comparable start-ups that have come a little further than you, to show that your figures are realistic and not pulled out of thin air.

5) **Reach widely**. Go on stage and pitch to a room full of investors; use online forums such as Angellist; canvass with the same fervour as when you're looking for customers and partners. Investors are just as unpredictable as the rest of us (i.e. human beings), so don't try to guess who's going to like your project. Give everyone a chance to fall in love.

6) But ... **beware of distractions**. There are wannabe investors out there who just want a free dinner and to hear about exciting projects. Make a habit of asking very quickly: 'What was the last investment you made?' If it was more

than two years ago and for a smaller amount than you are after, then pull out politely. You are an entrepreneur hunting for capital; don't pose as free entertainment.

7) Be proactive, **push the process continuously**. You are the one who needs money, and you cannot expect investors to do the work for you. It is you who must call them frequently, tell them about the progress since you last spoke, and bring the dialogue one step closer to a signature.

Raising capital will always be a disturbance in your efforts to achieve optimal efficiency. It is a large and in many cases unfamiliar task. You have to be your own timekeeper and design a process that leads to success without too many detours.

TIME SAVER #12:
BE SMART ABOUT RAISING MONEY

#13 DON'T LET TECHNOLOGY CONTROL YOU

BY JORDAN MILNE

Technology can be an efficient tool and a luxury that fosters flexibility. It can also trap you. There are no warning labels when you buy a new smartphone or log onto Facebook. No sticker that speaks of the addiction or time loss that can occur with their misuse.

In the modern world you can work every hour of the day. You can wake up in the middle of the night and go to the computer to work on whatever pops into your head. The potential is enormous, but you need to take control and be deliberate in your use of technology and communication tools. Don't let them control you.

Nowhere is this more dangerous than with email. Millions of us have read the international bestseller *The 4-Hour Workweek*, where Tim Ferriss threw a much-needed and well-aimed punch at email. Since the book hit the shelves, however, email has not dwindled sheepishly into the background. Far from it. According to recent research an overwhelming 96% of respondents report their email use has either stayed the same or increased in the past year, while a further 96% say they expect their work email use to stay the same or increase in the next 5 years. Until someone comes up with a real alternative, email is here to stay, and we have to make the best of it.

Stever Robbins, business coach and expert in efficiency, elaborates on the dangers of email misuse, and points towards at least three problems with it:

1) It draws our attention away from the task at hand and the people around us by luring us in with a false sense of urgency. We need to realise that – most of the time – if we don't answer our email immediately we are not going to miss a great opportunity or a huge problem that won't still be there later.

2) Your life is what happens while you're away from the computer, not while you're at the computer. Think about the best times in your life. Were you writing emails? Probably not.

3) Email also puts you in a reactive role instead of a proactive one: answering what other people want and can't find. Email has been described as a never-ending to-do list that someone else makes for you.

Spending time cleaning up your inbox is fine as a residual activity but the core of your time should be spent on your Wildly Important stuff. Be aware. Take control.

> ## TIME SAVER #13:
> ## DON'T BE A SLAVE TO YOUR EMAILS

#14 BE A BUSINESS PACIFIST

BY MARTIN BJERGEGAARD

Nelson Mandela, Mahatma Gandhi and the current Dalai Lama are three of the most influential and respected leaders in modern history. They are leaders from different countries and different eras, but they have one thing in common; they believe in peace, forgiveness and collaboration. One of Gandhi's famous quotes is: 'An eye for an eye makes the whole world blind.'

Fortunately it has been a long time since the Western world has experienced war, in the traditional sense, on home soil. We do not have to fear soldiers in our streets or bombs raining from the sky.

A very different type of war is still being fought, however, in our boardrooms and courtrooms. While this type of warfare cannot be compared to military conflict it is nevertheless more expensive and destructive today than it has ever been.

In 2008, American entrepreneurs paid $105 billion in litigation expenses, and that number rose to a stunning $152 billion in 2011. That figure is higher than the average annual US military spend during the Vietnam War.

The majority of conflicts in the corporate world do not escalate into courtroom trials. However, conflicts that play out discreetly within the corridors of lawyers' offices are no less expensive or stressful for those involved.

Consider the work-related conflicts you have experienced yourself: maybe a hard-fought battle between two company founders; a strike caused by distrust between management and staff; or perhaps investors who rip and tear at both ends of a company. The small battles we fight on a daily basis eat into our energy, waste our time and drain our cash.

Many start-ups suffer an early death thanks to these types of wars. We need more Mandelas, Gandhis and Dalai Lamas in the corporate world. Gandhi also encouraged us to 'be the change you want to see in the world'.

My hope is that you and I can make that change by becoming 'business pacifists'. Doing so will not only foster a deeper sense of peace in ourselves and create increased prosperity in the world, but will also make us both richer and happier.

We might be thinking: 'We have to protect ourselves when we are attacked.' But the definition and interpretation of attack varies drastically. Some people's threshold is so low that they are ready to fight if you look at them the wrong way. Others will endure many conscious insults before their pulse rises. The same applies in business. Our tolerance is determined by our self-esteem and personal maturity as well as whether we define ourselves based on what others think or do to us, or whether our sense of self comes from within.

Even if we are indisputably attacked we still have the freedom to choose our response. Not too long ago at Rainmaking we were faced with this decision when a former business partner recruited people from our staff, ripped off one of our companies' website, tried to poach an important supplier and started competing directly with us.

This was an overt breach of the agreement he himself had accepted when we initially bought him out of the company in question at the fair price he asked for. It was a huge personal disappointment because we really liked the man and thought the feeling was reciprocated. Maybe it was – there could have been many motives at play; maybe his wife had pushed him. She got a job in his new company.

Together our team discussed what an appropriate response might be. We would have done well in court, but we chose not to expend negative energy on it. In addition to energy, a trial would have taken time and money. Instead we decided to focus on putting those resources to use in bettering our own company. With this in mind we simply forgave him and got on with business.

This course of action worked incredibly well and later we made a successful multimillion exit of the business, while our former partner never really managed to prosper with his venture.

His failure could be attributed to many things, but personally I believe he never really had his heart in it. It feels wrong to copy others and violate agreements and it is certainly not the right starting point for something as demanding as launching a new start-up. His heart and energy worked against him instead of with him.

On the other hand we maintained our 'innocence', using our time, money and energy efficiently. What's more, a weight was lifted from our shoulders when we chose the path of forgiveness and generosity. It felt good.

Business pacifists can achieve big results. Like Gandhi, we will discover that turning the other cheek can be the most powerful response of all. Though painful in the short term, in the long run it is more than likely to crush the aggressor standing before us, making us a role model and inspiring others to do the same.

It is easy to impulsively become fascinated by aggression, perhaps inspired by action films and books. But who are the people who win and keep our admiration and respect in the long run? They are the ones who show us love and compassion, not the ones who bully others with aggression.

TIME SAVER #14:
AVOID UNNECESSARY CONFLICTS

WHEN THE ROAD IS ROUGH

So you have chosen to be an entrepreneur or a business leader. Welcome to a path as bumpy as an African village road. To put it frankly, all of us will need to fasten our mental seatbelts, otherwise our healthy sense of humour and lust for life will not be able to make the journey with us. We will encounter setbacks, defeats and failures – some of which will seem fatal.

But they are not. When we are entrepreneurs there is no such thing as a failure – only experience of different feedback. We need to keep going, we need to be masters of the comeback. It sounds brutal, but it doesn't have to be. It is all in your mind. The next five essays will help you to stay strong and even cheerful when the heat is on or the valley is deep.

#1 LOVE YOUR STAIRS

BY MARTIN BJERGEGAARD

Have you ever noticed how people prepare themselves for retirement? Talking about moving to a one-storey house, so they can avoid those 'nasty stairs'? Or about how they are looking forward to retiring so they never again have to worry about setting an alarm clock? Many people start thinking these thoughts when they approach their 60s, and some even earlier.

When my father started approaching 60, he made three decisions, all of which I, at the time, strongly disagreed with and from which I tried to dissuade him. He turned down an offer to sell his investment property for a nice sum of money, and instead embarked on a comprehensive renovation and development project of the same property – a project which put his finances in jeopardy, and which has kept him busy to this day. Secondly, at 56 years of age, he joined the local karate club – he turned up one day with his white belt and grey hair and started exchanging stroke series with his new 20-year-old peers. And thirdly, as a 59 year old, he had another son, my little brother Krystian, who today is 7 years old and a great playmate to my 5-year-old daughter.

'A man scared sick of getting old,' was my thought, and honestly, I felt badly for him. But today, at 66, I have to note that my father hasn't aged a day in the last 10 years. Sure, he has a couple of extra wrinkles, but in all important respects he is doing much better than most 50 year olds. He exercises twice a day and is in better physical shape than I am. When we lift weights together, I have to accept defeat, and every time it takes me by surprise. He speaks like a young man, hangs out in the karate club, and likes to discuss website functionalities. But the most important thing is that he is happy and healthy and he still gets as much out of every day as he did back when he was 30.

Most of my father's friends of the same age aren't much fun to be around these days. They retired a couple of years ago and spend their time sitting still and talking about the weather. They are quickly relieving themselves of the last small challenges in life; getting rid of the stairs, hiring someone else to cut the garden hedge and selling the summer cottage because it is too much work. In other words, they are doing all they can to dismantle what was once their lives.

Life coach Anthony Robbins inspires us by telling stories of those who, in their old age, are still living their lives to the fullest. 'The good life' does not necessarily come from achieving a lot and then suddenly ceasing to achieve anything at all. The dream of early retirement is a lie. **Happiness is about keeping active and always embarking on new challenges, which allow you to learn and grow**.

This insight holds enormous potential for us entrepreneurs. Many of us dream of scoring the big bucks, and we can be disappointed and disillusioned if success doesn't come when we hope or expect it to. There is, however, no reason for us to feel this way. The most important thing for our happiness is that we continue to prioritise it, are constantly learning new things, and maintain our appetite for life. Contrary to what we might expect, these real, more inner, goals are actually easier to achieve without having $100 million in your bank account and servants catering to your every whim. Enjoy the challenges that life and your entrepreneurial projects present to you.

EMPOWERING THOUGHT #1:
TROUBLE = CHALLENGES =
GROWTH = HAPPINESS

#2 SPOT OPPORTUNITY IN DANGER

BY JORDAN MILNE

For most of us, balance feels achievable when things are going well. When travelling along a road that is straight and smooth we can switch on the cruise control, let the windows down and enjoy the ride.

When all goes as planned, people find it easier to fit some form of balance into their lives. We don't mind leaving the office early when business is great or taking extra holidays to celebrate good earnings or a new deal.

The reality is that things rarely do go as planned. So what happens when plans misfire? This is when our commitment to balance is truly tested. When an unanticipated challenge arises it can throw our life into a tailspin. Whether in our business or personal life, it can knock us off course and off centre. Many of us get stressed and some never fully recover.

Sophie Vandebroek, CTO at XEROX, has overcome adversity and has a thing or two to say about it. Her strength lies not only in her ability to achieve balance and success on good days, but in her ability to maintain a positive outlook and keep that balance in the face of hardship, like when her husband tragically died. Sophie takes a cue from her favourite proverb, *In danger there is opportunity.*

Sophie explains: 'It [danger] is a Chinese word with two strokes: danger and chaos. At first glance it's a scary word, but if you cover the left stroke and look at the right stroke it says opportunity. Having the mindset of always looking at the opportunity, no matter how bad your situation, has proven very valuable for me. For example, if a competitor comes in right before you're going to launch your new product or some of your experiments fail. Or at home, if you break up with your boyfriend or you experience a tragedy like 9/11, or worse, someone you love dies, it's definitely understandable to be hurt and scared.

'Many people, however, get paralysed. When people hear there are lay-offs happening in their company they freeze. I always tell them this is an opportunity. Work on your résumé, offer proposals on how to do things differently, go out and help those who are in need. Make new friends if you break up. There is so much opportunity out there if you can recondition yourself. Looking at the opportunities and not the dangers helps you to achieve balance. Although it is sometimes hard to do, once you make the mental shift you will begin to reflexively ask yourself, OK what is the opportunity here?'

Whatever the size or type of obstacle you encounter, try not only to make the best of it, but actively seek out the opportunities it brings. What is the biggest challenge you face today? How can you flip it on its head?

EMPOWERING THOUGHT #2:
EACH SETBACK IS A NEW OPPORTUNITY

#3 REMEMBER THERE IS ALWAYS A WAY

BY MARTIN BJERGEGAARD

When success doesn't come as easy as they would like, some are all too quick to blame their circumstances and surroundings. Success would be possible if, and only if, the odds hadn't been so heavily stacked against them. Maxim Spiridonov represents a refreshing change from this mentality. His story and his attitude illustrate what is possible.

At our interview, 34-year-old Maxim speaks in a calm and confident manner about his favourite business ventures. One of them publishes two Russian web magazines, each with approximately 100,000 users. Another is a business podcast site, the best known in Russia, which he started in 2008. Today he has sold half of the business to a Moscow-based VC firm and has inked a deal with the Russian version of *Forbes* magazine to publish their podcasts in text form.

Maxim hasn't limited himself to the media industry. His newest start-up is a software program for buying and selling foreign currencies. When I met him, this business had been going for only 8 months and had already grown to 40 employees: programmers, analysts, risk managers, dealers. They generate revenue by charging a fee for every transaction, and are impressively enough already profitable.

Maxim looks fit as he sits there in his black T-shirt. Even though it feels awkward, in the name of my mission I muster up the courage to ask him if he works out often. 'Yes, 30–40 minutes of daily morning exercise, stretching and yoga,' is his easy response, which indicates that I might have managed to hide my embarrassment. 'Plus two to three times a week at the gym.' Actually, he is going to the gym after the interview. How does he get the time?

'I don't have time not to keep fit. Being healthy is the foundation for success.' I get the idea that this is something he has said before, perhaps to his co-founders and colleagues, or maybe at his frequent lectures at entrepreneurship events. There, his favourite message is about the importance of creating trusting, respectful and mutually enriching relationships with your partners and colleagues. 'It's really all about trust,' is his favourite saying.

Maxim spent the entire month of January in Thailand. 'It doesn't matter where I live, just as long as there is a reliable Internet connection,' he explains. The last 3 months have taken him on trips to Israel, Ukraine and Switzerland, in addition to tours of his vast homeland, including one to Siberia. Next stop is a trip to Turkey with his two daughters. They are 9 and 12 years old, and have their base in Nuremberg, Germany, with their mother. The time Maxim doesn't spend travelling he splits evenly between his businesses in Moscow and his daughters in Nuremberg. It works fine, and Maxim enjoys the fact that in this way he is integrated into two cultures simultaneously.

It all seems a little too easy, and I start getting suspicious. Are his parents possibly among those oligarchs I have read about in the newspapers? Was he born with a silver spoon in his mouth?

None of these speculations are close to the truth. Maxim has earned every rouble he owns. He was originally educated as an actor, trying to scratch a living in the theatres of St Petersburg. When he started a family, he needed to bring home more money than the acting profession could provide him with. It was 1998, and a crisis of historic proportions shook the foundations of the new Russian market economy.

In my conversations with him, Maxim does not mention a single word about the crisis. Nor does he mention the fact that it was difficult to get started as an entrepreneur without capital, without the relevant contacts or the right education. It does not seem to be a part of his way of looking at the world. Instead, he talks about how he and some friends from the theatre started a company organising events: 'We knew about showbiz, and had lots of contacts who could help us set up some amazing events. We enjoyed it so much that for us it was a game more than a business. We reached a turnover of 4 to 5 million US dollars a year and in 2004 I sold my share and moved to Germany to try something new.'

'Doing business is about having fun,' says Maxim, and it sounds like another one of his mottos.

A few years ago, he created a social community, where people could vote on who they thought should be the next president of Russia. It was thought of as a practical joke, but it attracted thousands of participants and lots of publicity. Next month he is starting tango lessons with his girlfriend.

'He is one of the most famous young IT entrepreneurs in Moscow,' my Russian contact tells me later, as we push our way onto the subway that transports as many people as the subways of London and New York combined; 8 million people a day, half the population of Europe's biggest city.

I understand why Maxim is so popular. His story and his charisma made an equally strong impression on me. How often do we meet people of potential who hold themselves back because they lack money, live in the wrong country, are in the middle of a crisis, have the wrong education, are too young or too old, lack an idea, or don't know the right people?

Maxim reminds us of what we all know but often forget; that there is always a way. And that the only necessary prerequisite is the ability to see possibilities instead of limitations.

> ## EMPOWERING THOUGHT #3:
> ## REGARDLESS OF YOUR CURRENT SITUATION, WINNING WITHOUT LOSING IS POSSIBLE FOR YOU

#4 MAKE MANY ATTEMPTS

BY MARTIN BJERGEGAARD

In 2008, Derek Sivers sold his online music shop CD Baby for $22 million. He is invited to speak at TED conferences and has been featured in such high-profile magazines as *Wired* and *Esquire*. Recently he published a bestselling book, *Anything you Want*, detailing 40 lessons about entrepreneurship. NBC has described him as 'revolutionising the music business'.

As if this weren't enough, Derek also has a reputation for living a balanced life. He complied with our request to interview him, but on one condition; we were to ask our questions in writing so he could answer them in his own time: perhaps an indication of his commitment to using his time wisely. One of the first questions we asked Derek was pure and simple: 'Why are you so successful?' Only a few minutes later, we got an answer. It was honest, precise and left a lasting impression.

'Just luck,' he said. 'I started CD Baby at exactly the right time, with just the right services. I've started a dozen other businesses that didn't take off, but for some reason that one did,' he continued.

To my surprise, Derek didn't have a clue why CD Baby had become a success. He even resisted the temptation to do some after-the-fact rationalisation. Instead, he shared the truth with us.

He was unable to see the difference between the dozens of projects that ended up in 'the start-up cemetery', and CD Baby, which had turned him into a superstar entrepreneur and cemented his status as an idol to thousands of independent musicians.

McKinsey & Co., mentioned earlier in this book, is recognised as one of the leading consulting firms in the world. McKinsey's people are hailed as some of the sharpest, most analytical brains on the planet. When the most powerful companies and governments need help, they call McKinsey. Towards the end of the 1990s, McKinsey decided to enter the start-up scene. Instead of billing their usual 'monster fees', they wanted to work alongside entrepreneurs in return for equity in their start-ups. It became sensational; offices dedicated to this new concept shot up around the world. Many of the greatest minds in business bought into the idea. Three years later it was all closed down and millions of dollars were lost.

What went wrong for this highly respected consultancy firm? While there were undoubtedly many causes, first and foremost was a fundamental preconception: McKinsey thought that they could pick the winners. They thought that with their experience, methods and brains, they could read through hundreds of business plans and pick out the few that had the potential to be an international success. They were wrong. Their estimates turned out no better than yours or mine. Just like Derek Sivers, they had no clue what would sail and what would sink.

Why is it so hard to predict a successful model? The explanation is

pretty simple. There are just too many unknown factors in entrepreneurship; making predictions is a fool's errand. A much-cited
example is Tom Watson's famous estimate of the market for computers when, as CEO of IBM, he assessed the total global demand
for computers to be no more than five. McKinsey once opined that
mobile phones would be a 'niche' market. And who can forget
Bill Gates's self-assured answer in 1993, when he was asked about
Microsoft's view on the Internet, which was gaining ground at the
time: 'The Internet? We are not interested in it.' **When people as
smart as Tom Watson and Bill Gates and firms such as McKinsey can be so wrong, it's a clear indication of how difficult it is
to predict success**.

So if no one can assess entrepreneurial outcomes with any meaningful degree of predictability, then what is the best way to pro-
ceed? The answer is simple. Try many times. Try many ideas,
many projects and many start-ups. To have only one or two tickets
in the raffle is too few. Like Derek, you want to have at least ten
shots at success, and preferably even more.

I once read about a telemarketing salesman who figured out that
his hit rate was 5%. So for every 20 people he called, he got an
order. He made it a habit to celebrate every time he got a rejec-
tion, because then he was one call closer to a sale. This man might
sound crazy to us, but he delivered the top results in his company. When you accept the fact that you may have to make several
attempts to find a winner, then it's easier to lean back and enjoy
the ride. Then, every time you find yourself in a checkmate position or have to close down a project, it is no longer a failure but

a valuable learning experience – and you are that one important step closer to hitting the jackpot.

EMPOWERING THOUGHT #4:
IT IS ALL ABOUT MAKING MANY ATTEMPTS
(AND PERSEVERING ON THE RIGHT ONES)

#5 KNOW THAT IT IS NEVER TOO LATE

BY JORDAN MILNE

Mark Zuckerberg (Facebook) and Andrew Mason (Groupon) reached their billionaire status while in their 20s. In an era when founders seem to get younger by the day it is easy to think that once you're over 35, you're over the hill.

Although the success of these entrepreneurs is impressive and certainly makes for great press, they are of course the exception rather than the rule. The evidence suggests that most entrepreneurs can indeed keep improving as they get older and more experienced. Don't get caught in the negative belief that your physical, mental and creative faculties deteriorate at the speed so many have accepted as reality. **It is never too late to achieve success doing something you love**.

To find inspiration in athletics one need look no further than the new poster boy for Adidas: Fauja Singh, a 100-year-old marathon runner. In India, when he was 84 years old, his wife and youngest son died, and Singh moved to the UK to live with his other son. Fighting homesickness, loneliness and boredom, Singh found solace in jogging. Gradually, running became his passion and joy, and at the age of 89 he ran his first marathon.

In the arts, think of the American painter Anna Mary Robertson

Moses. When her arthritis grew too severe for her to continue embroidering she took up painting. She was 76 years old. Today her paintings hang in museums all over the world, as well as in the White House. In 2006 her painting *Sugaring Off* sold for $1.2 million. When grandma Moses died at the age of 101 she had painted over 3,600 paintings in what has become recognised as a folk-style uniquely her own.

In politics there is Hazel 'The Hurricane' McCallion, who at 90 years of age became the mayor of Mississauga, Canada. Her no-nonsense attitude garnered her 76% of the votes.

Colonel Harland Sanders launched his business at the age of 65, using his first social security cheque as seed capital. He hit the road to peddle his 'secret recipe fried chicken' to restaurants and, when he died at the age of 90, his world famous Kentucky Fried Chicken chain already had 6,000 outlets with sales of more than $2 billion. When Ray Kroc took on the first McDonald's franchise, buying out the original founders and going on to grow it into the giant that it is today, he was already in his 50s.

Examples abound in every field of human endeavour. Moses and Singh, McCallion, Sanders and Kroc are testament to the fact that it is never too late to achieve greatness in your respective field. So shed the disagreeable notion that your best years are behind you. The best ones are those you are about to live, and the very best day to get started is today.

EMPOWERING THOUGHT #5:
PEOPLE OLDER (AND YOUNGER)
THAN YOU ARE STARTING UP THEIR
FIRST BUSINESS TODAY

BALANCE BY DESIGN

→ 10 WAYS TO STOP HOPING FOR IT
AND START PLANNING FOR IT

When we create something physical we usually start by designing it. Whether it's a garage, a doll's house or a bridge. You wouldn't just start out in one corner and hope for the best. Of course, we all try to design our start-ups as well – that's called a business plan. We think about business models, organisation, products and revenue projections. Maybe we even try to plan and control these factors too much, as we have discussed in an earlier essay. But there is one question that very few entrepreneurs remember to factor in at the design phase: **How do I structure this business so that it will allow me and my team a good balance?**

It's an obvious question, isn't it? If balance is closely connected to quality of life, then why would you forget to optimise it alongside your venture's other key performance indicators? Most entrepreneurs would love to do so, but miss the inspiration and awareness to be 'designers of balance'. Here are 10 essays to change that.

#1 BUILD WITH BALANCE IN MIND

BY JORDAN MILNE

Chad Troutwine has an infectious energy about him. He leaves a lasting impression on everyone he meets. When you talk to him you get the feeling that you are the only person in the world. His confidence shines through in every situation. 'If you ask my friends, they'd tell you I have a healthy level of confidence,' says Chad. His lust for life is evident. He has charm.

As mentioned in an earlier essay, Chad is the co-founder of Veritas Prep, a company he started with his friend Markus in grad school. Together they entered and won many business plan competitions. While other students were pitching businesses with blue ocean strategies, Chad was focusing on execution. 'We knew we could make a better mousetrap,' he says. Veritas now brings in roughly $15 million per annum. What's even more impressive is that because of the way they scaled the business Chad and Markus never had to take on outside investors – meaning they own 100% of the company.

Veritas Prep offers test preparation courses and tutoring, both in person and online. Their customers are students eager to get into a top school for their MBA programme. Veritas helps them learn the material effectively so that they don't have to spend all of their time studying, can go and have a beer with their friends and still get into the school of their dreams.

When not running Veritas, Chad may be at the premiere of one of his films at Cannes or Sundance, spending time with friends, travelling or working on one of his many 'passion projects'. The ten films he has so far invested in have featured actors such as James Woods, Christina Ricci, Vince Vaughn and Natalie Portman and world-renowned directors such as Joel and Ethan Coen.

Most recently Chad produced the film version of the bestselling book *Freakonomics* and joined Stephen J. Dubner and Steven D. Levitt to form Freakonomics Media, LLC in 2011. Chad also enjoys playing basketball, tennis and squash and practising mixed martial arts. You might think that with all this going on, it would be tough to get a meeting with Chad inside the next 6 months. But because of the way Chad has designed his business and his life that is not the case.

'I'm always the one in my group of friends who is available. If someone says, I want to go to London or Costa Rica and next week is the only time, I'm in,' he says, with a smile that makes me feel he is reminiscing about his last adventure.

If you think Chad has created this life for himself on the backs of others, think again. Chad is not the kind of co-founder who lets his partner work tirelessly by candlelight so that he can explore the world and pursue his passions. Quite the opposite. His business partner Markus Moberg often works 3 days a week and spends much of his free time travelling. The last two times we spoke to Markus he was returning from his adventures; a safari in Africa and snowboarding in Japan. Markus was born in Sweden and grew up in Norway. He was on his way to Wall Street when Chad convinced him to try his hand at entrepreneurship instead.

Veritas was built on a simple premise with a clever approach. Chad and Markus took a model that had been proven to be effective by their competitors, tweaked a few elements to give them an advantage and then carried out flawless execution. They put the stress on both quality and quantity: their course is twice as long as those of their competitors and all of their teachers have scored in the 99th percentile themselves on the tests they teach. To keep the costs down, Veritas forms partnerships with universities to use buildings on campus instead of renting pricey buildings in the city. Veritas gets prime locations with easy access to their demographic, and the schools get a great service for their students.

Win–win.

Chad figures he is able to have his success as well as the time and energy to enjoy it by not settling for less than his initial vision.

'**Veritas was built from the start with balance in mind**,' Chad explains. 'There are a lot of variables at play in selecting business opportunities, and you want to make sure they all match up to what you're looking for. Veritas was designed to be scalable and self-sustaining. Markus and I had a very clear vision of what we wanted to create: a hugely successful business that was fun, efficient, involved great people, ran like clockwork, made large profits AND availed us the time to relax and spend time on other things we were passionate about. I didn't want to construct a prison for myself,' he continues.

Often we entrepreneurs do exactly that: we choose a business that severely limits our freedom, and we don't even think twice about it. Chad and Markus remind us to factor in our balance and happiness as early as the evaluation and design phase.

DESIGN ELEMENT #1: PICK A BUSINESS THAT'S SUITABLE FOR BALANCE

#2 PREPARE YOURSELF

BY MARTIN BJERGEGAARD

What do you do better than most other people? Swimming, cooking or maybe playing bridge? You may well have been born with talents, but, unless you have supernatural powers, practice was surely a defining factor.

The same goes for building your business; you have to practise and you have to be prepared.

The five founders of Fullrate, which turned out to be the success story of the year in Denmark in 2009, are the most prepared entrepreneurs I have ever come across. As former employees at the market leader they had done almost exactly what they set out to do again as entrepreneurs; create a broadband company from scratch.

Back in 2005, a company called CyberCity was the leading broadband provider in Denmark, riding high and ruling the market. Comfortable in its position, top management did not see any reason to implement the new technology appearing in the market. Therefore Peter, Stig, Haktan, Nicolai and Kasper disappeared out the front door and never returned.

Instead they created the phenomenon called Fullrate; a rocket start-up launching cheap broadband for the people. Within 3 years they signed a $75 million exit to the old phone monopolist in Denmark, TDC.

Looking back, their fate seems predestined. At CyberCity, Haktan had built IT systems, Peter had acquired customers, Nicolai had taken care of finances, Stig had done strategy and Kasper knew the technology inside out.

All the important competences were gathered within the team. They trusted each other and delivered the same service as they had done in previous years, only cheaper and more efficiently.

But it does not necessarily take years to prepare for your next project. English super-entrepreneur Peter Jones, known from the TV phenomenon *Dragons Den*, writes in his book *Tycoon* about how at the age of 19–20 he worked for a couple of years in various computer companies in different positions, to learn as much as possible about the industry before he went on to create his own business.

His plan worked and he managed to create a successful business in record time.

You do not have to be an industry expert to be successful. Too many years of preparation can hinder your ability to act and think creatively. But a year or two absorbing knowledge is a good idea, whether you want to work with broadband or computers or something entirely different.

DESIGN ELEMENT #2:

FIGURE OUT HOW TO ACQUIRE THE SKILLS TO

BE PREPARED FOR YOUR NEXT VENTURE

#3 REVISIT 8-8-8

BY JORDAN MILNE

Some say that life is not fair. That statement is true on many counts, but there is one constant. No matter where you were born, where you went to school, who your parents are or what your favourite flavour of ice cream is, everyone gets 24 hours in a day. Count 'em: 24.

Meet Mitch Thrower. Mitch is by any measure an exceptional individual and is truly someone who squeezes the most out of life. He is an author, financier, entrepreneur and 22-time Ironman triathlete, as well as the only photojournalist to photograph and video the Ironman Triathlon World Championships while doing the event.

For those of you unfamiliar with it, the Ironman is the pinnacle of endurance races. It is a gruelling test of fitness and willpower, which most triathletes consider it a career highlight just to finish. An Ironman sees those brave enough to step up to the challenge complete a 2.4-mile (3.86-km) swim followed by a 112-mile (180.25-km) bike ride. As if that weren't enough, participants then run a marathon (26 miles, 385 yards – 42.195km). Training for these races requires true dedication, and often takes a tremendous toll on other aspects of a trainee's life.

'I've met people who have given up their jobs, cars, homes, and ultimately their significant others for the opportunity to line up in the shallow waters of Kailua Bay with 1,600 of their closest triathlon friends. I've also met people who have enhanced their jobs and relationships thanks to Ironman,' Mitch shares, thereby giving us a first taste of what he believes to be possible.

In the business arena, Mitch is just as accomplished. He is a prolific serial entrepreneur and has co-founded several successful sports-related companies, one of them The Active Network, which has evolved into the de facto international standard for online sports registration and payments, processing more than 70 million transactions yearly. And through Thrower Ventures, Mitch's investment company, he has invested in more than a dozen flourishing start-ups and projects.

So Mitch must spend all of his time and energy on his athletics and businesses, then?

Not so. He also takes time to give back to society and is heavily involved in philanthropy and social ventures. He is chairman of the La Jolla Foundation, which runs a non-profit programme providing finance, mentoring, sports and education to war-torn locations. Their latest initiative saw soccer balls and jerseys given to the children of Afghanistan, Haiti and Iraq.

Mitch is also an avid writer. He has authored the book *The Attention Deficit Workplace* and has been a columnist for *Triathlete Magazine* and *BizSanDiego*.

So how does Mitch get all this done? How does he accomplish more day after day than so many would ever consider possible? Mitch builds multimillion-dollar businesses, stays in peak physical condition, writes books, helps underprivileged children through the power of sport and still finishes up the day with a smile on his face.

One of his secrets lies in a simple time management principle that he learned from a man named Schott Tinley. An author, teacher and two-time Ironman Hawaii champion, Tinley was one of the most powerful forces in the sport of triathlon in the 1980s and is an Ironman Hall-of-Famer.

Mitch told us that something Schott Tinley said would stay with him for ever: you have 8 hours in the day to work, and another 8 hours in the day for you to sleep – and rarely does anybody sleep for a full 8 hours. After all this you then still have 8 hours for yourself. 'So, he had this 8–8-8 rule and once I realised it was true, I became excited to think of all the possibilities the rule of 8 presented every day to a dedicated person. **You just have to control the 8 hours which are yours and not get caught in the slippery slope of time-wasting detours.**'

So when you are looking at all the things you want to accomplish and feel overwhelmed, remember that everyone gets 24 hours in a day: Mitch Thrower, Einstein, Rockefeller, Oprah, Richard Branson and you. Use them wisely and you have more than enough time.

DESIGN ELEMENT #3:
SPLIT UP AND PROTECT YOUR DAY,
DON'T LET WORK TAKE IT ALL OVER

#4 Build Back-up Systems

By Jordan Milne

You're an airline operating out of London's Heathrow, the second busiest airport in the world and the hub that handles the most international traffic. You wake up to one of the most severe snowstorms in recent memory.

Suddenly, all flights are cancelled and thousands are left stranded. The calls start coming in and the losses start piling up. It feels like a dam has broken and there is water pouring in at breakneck speed.

You're an entrepreneur working on a partnership proposal with a large firm that is due in the morning. You get up to get a snack and return to your laptop only to find that your 2-year-old child has poured milk all over it.

What do you do?

What will you do if your system breaks? Many are prepared for what they think will happen. **It takes a specific kind of preparation to get ready for what you fear will happen**. It could be something as simple as backing up your files. Putting these systems in place means that you are one step closer to preventing a catastrophe. Doing so will affect not only your success, but also your stress levels and your time.

Stever Robbins's prior experience as an entrepreneur, business coach and engineer drove home the importance of having back-up systems. To this day it has influenced him to develop back-up systems in his own ventures as well as in the ventures of those he coaches.

'If you don't know how you're going to recover if your service breaks, it's like painting a big red target on yourself. And that will eventually result in you having to do a lot more work and having an unbalanced life,' Stever says.

Stever has been an adviser and mentor to many senior managers in high-growth companies. He often encounters intelligent entrepreneurs who have thought thoroughly about all areas except for having a back-up plan:

'I was recently working with an entrepreneur who was raising money. I asked him what he was going to do if he couldn't raise the money. He said that wasn't an option. He had no plan B. To which I responded that it wasn't under his control. Not every business in the world needs to be capitalised with millions of dollars right out of the gate. You can get vendor financing. You can take on a volunteer or you can trade equity for manufacturing. There are all kinds of solutions, but if you're going to wait until after your financing falls apart to decide what your next steps are going to be that's just stupid,' Stever says.

'The ticket to having a balanced life is having a life that's predictable enough to put the balance into it. It's not going to be predictable unless you build systems that are reasonably resilient and have back-ups so that if one thing fails another can pick up the slack,' he continues.

Maybe you have already taken the critical steps necessary to protect your business. But Stever takes this ethos one step further and applies it to the rest of his life. His interests include swing dancing, comedy improvisation and hypnosis – and he's learned that even zombies need back-up systems.

'I'm in this play and I'm playing a zombie. Last night my pants got caught – the fake blood that we're using is very sticky and there's a moment when I have to crawl behind a prop on the stage so that I can jump up later and be scary. As I was crawling the sticky blood on the stage caught on my pants and it tore them all the way up. Had I not been wearing underwear we would have been having an X-rated moment. Tonight I'm bringing a spare pair of pants! Do I expect to tear my pants? No, but now I'm bringing a back-up system so that just in case there's a problem, I'll be ready to keep going,' Stever explains.

If things don't go as planned but you have the necessary back-up in place, then what might have been a failure simply becomes plan B. A dead end turns into an alternate route. There will always be things you can't control, but by taking precautions you can influence the effect these events will have on your business, helping you to maintain control and balance even under difficult circumstances.

DESIGN ELEMENT #4: THINK AHEAD TO SECURE YOUR FUTURE BALANCE

#5 IMPROVE YOUR OUTSIDE/INSIDE RATIO

Sitting inside, moment after moment, can take its toll. Just as we were not meant to stay still all day, neither are we meant to stay caged up inside. We spend long days at the office and then hop into a car and drive home, living most of our lives within the man-made physical forms we have created. If you are like most people then your outside/inside (O/I) ratio is heavily tilted to the 'I' side. It used not to be like this and we're not quite sure how we got here. I haven't met anyone who aspires to this lifestyle, yet most live it. On average, Americans spend over 90% of their time indoors. For most entrepreneurs, the percentage is even greater.

Disruptive ideas happen when we think outside the box and amazing lives happen when we actually go outside the box. Which would you prefer: artificial light and stale air; or natural light, the smell of nature and fresh air? When was the last time you took a minute to actually look up at the sky? Not hurry along from the office to your train or your car, but purposefully, consciously, take a moment to enjoy the outside? It may feel contrived at first, but it does wonders. The positive effects that being outside have on your body are well documented. The sun provides us with much-needed vitamin D, which, as long as exposure isn't excessive, can help prevent cancer and bone disease and control insulin levels. The sunlight makes our brain produce natural hormones

BALANCE BY DESIGN / 195

that wake us up and make us feel more alert. Having even a short period of time outside also helps reset circadian rhythms and promotes weight loss. In the summertime these effects are heightened by a concentrated ratio of negative ions in the air that have been proven to boost our mood.

Think going outside only affects us in the moment? Not so. Research indicates that getting out into nature can help people's long-term recovery from stress and fatigue. Spending time outside can have a profound mental effect. Finding the time could be as simple as eating your lunch outside 3 days a week, having your meetings outdoors, walking to work, taking a phone call outside or even taking a few minutes to unabashedly relax and enjoy the sunshine. The richness and freshness of sensory input from outside not only perks up your mind but also gives you a sense of perspective by reminding you that there is a bigger world out there. If you don't have the time for an outdoor adventure, then at least step out for a quick breath of fresh air. In fact, put down this book and walk outside. Just for two minutes.

DESIGN ELEMENT #5:
ALWAYS HAVE ACCESS TO FRESH AIR

#6 PICK YOUR FAVOURITE LOCATION

BY JORDAN MILNE

In many businesses, notably real estate and retail, location has long been king. But things have evolved in the past 10 years and this truism is quite likely no longer the case for entrepreneurship in general.

Many ambitious entrepreneurs do, of course, feel the pressure to move to one of the world's major hubs of business, fuelled by a notion that it is from these places, and from these places only, that they can draw the inspiration, capital and contacts they need to make it big. But the reality is that we no longer need to live in Silicon Valley, New York City, London or Tokyo to have a fair shot at success. The rules that once made this so no longer apply. Moving to a business mecca is great, as long as you are sure you will enjoy the experience, but it is no longer necessary to sacrifice your home and location in order to succeed in business.

While these traditional business centres have their advantages they also have plenty of drawbacks. Setting up an Internet company in Silicon Valley in theory gives you easier access to high-calibre investors, but the landscape is also that much more competitive. Looking to set up an office in New York City? While this may bring you closer to a desirable and energised pool of talent, you will also be paying a premium for it. There are countless examples of successful companies that started off in relatively unknown cities.

Corydon (Indiana), Haiku (Hawaii) and Pendergrass (Georgia) play host to three of the fastest growing private companies in the United States: online appliance retailer Appliance Zone, photovoltaic cell producer Rising Sun, and frozen food packing company Signature Foods. Today, more than ever, it is possible to work from wherever you choose.

Jake Nickell, founder of Threadless, knows what he's looking for in a city and is not afraid to make a priority of his family and his passion for snowboarding when choosing where he lives, while running his revolutionary business.

Jake is a happy man. At first glance he looks more like a kid than a veteran CEO, but his appearance is a reflection of both his lifestyle and the fact that he is still just 30 years old. He has a wiry frame with tousled blond hair and is reserved and polite, but speaks very directly, like a man with nothing to hide.

Typically, Jake works less than 8 hours a day and lives with his wife and young daughter in Boulder, Colorado, a city famous for its active lifestyle and great outdoor activities. He loves getting out, enjoying the fresh air and all that Boulder has to offer. If you call his office in the late afternoon you may just find that Jake is out carving perfect turns in fresh powder down the mountainside on his snowboard. Family is really important to him, so he has created a lifestyle for himself where he can easily cater to it.

This is not as difficult as it might sound. Have you ever felt like uprooting and moving to the perfect city, but worried that your business might fail if you do? Jake moved from Chicago, where Threadless is based, to Boulder because he preferred the lifestyle and wanted to raise his family there. Quite a move for someone who is running a multimillion-dollar business. He also credits the move as the root of much of his happiness. It has allowed him to raise his family in a fun and safe environment while keeping him close to the slopes and trails.

How has he managed to create such an ideal lifestyle for himself? Jake is a great example of someone who uses all the tools available to him to run his satellite office successfully.

Although Boulder is now making a name for itself as a centre for innovation, Jake made his move when this movement was far less developed. His presence is now part of that movement, contributing to the city's rising stature in the entrepreneurial community.

Mitch Thrower, co-founder of The Active Network, also knows the importance of living somewhere you love.

'One key to balance and happiness is to find a place to live and work that is somewhere you actually want to be. I picked La Jolla, California, and then built an industry here,' Mitch tells us.

For Mitch, living somewhere with great weather and convenient access to the roads and water where he trains is paramount:

'It is paradise, and it's great to be able to work flexible hours when you know it's always nice outside and you can fit in workouts any time.'

When you are deciding where to live, take the complete picture into account. You can make a successful business nearly anywhere, so make the decision based on what's important to you, both personally and professionally. Maybe you give priority to being with friends or family? Maybe you want to be in the midst of a certain culture? Perhaps being able to do the activities you want is what will make you happiest? Decide where is the best fit for you instead of living where you think you should.

Danish entrepreneur Michael Bodekaer takes this aspiration to the next level. After having lived in many different parts of the world, he decided that Bali was the best place to suit his need for sun, kite surfing and adventure. After relocating, he wanted to give other entrepreneurs a taste for the same thing. Soon after, Project Getaway was born, a 6-week getaway for groups of 10 to 20 entrepreneurs, where they can have fun together while simultaneously launching start-ups from the comfort of beach chairs, sipping tropical drinks.

You might think that living beachside would reduce Michael's productivity. But this is not the case. He and his Getaway colleagues have launched several new companies as well as creating new business partnerships with local Indonesian business people.

Jake, Mitch and Michael are clear examples of how flexible location can be when it comes to business success. So if there is somewhere you've always wanted to live but thought your business couldn't survive there, think again. Living somewhere that excites you and makes you happy is good for business too.

DESIGN ELEMENT #6:
LIVE SOMEWHERE THAT EXCITES YOU

#7 ACHIEVE CRITICAL MASS

BY MARTIN BJERGEGAARD

The very first essay in this book was called 'Assemble your wheel' and it advised you to hook up with great co-founders, instead of going it alone. This is a message I share wherever I go to talk about entrepreneurship. However, I often get a response like: 'But it is so difficult to gather the right team, and to make it work day after day – tell me more about how to do that.' This essay and the following two elaborate on the topic of co-founders, which we have come to believe is the single most important factor in getting to winning without losing.

Imagine that you are looking to start a new company one week from today. Write a list of potential co-founders: people you trust, share values with and who have the right competences. People you can imagine being able to convince to leave their current job and form a new company and partnership.

How long is your list?

With Wikipedia, Facebook and Twitter, critical mass happens when you have enough users for it to become both fun and useful to take part. When it comes to co-founders, critical mass happens when you bring together enough qualified candidates to create a winning team. A list with 30 names is better than a list with 3, and you may need at least 10 candidates on your list before you can recruit even one or two. The hit rate is often as low as selling magazine subscriptions, so you need to make many calls.

If you are single and want a girlfriend or boyfriend, how do you increase your chances of hitting the jackpot? By being 'out there', attending parties, opening an online dating account, smiling at those you're interested in, talking, laughing and interacting. Co-founders are found in the same way. Except that you will need to exchange parties for networking events, and the online dating account turns into time spent on blogs and forums. The spark in the eye is replaced by energetic handshakes and the smile is adjusted 10 degrees from mysterious to trustworthy. In the end, however, it is all about putting yourself out there.

Even shy people find romantic partners, and just as there is a life partner for every one of us, there is also a co-founder for all entrepreneurs. Use just 10% of the energy you would normally spend on hunting for romance, and you'll find your co-founders before you can speak the words: 'Will you start a business with me?'

If you have difficulty finding the time, feel rejected or are finding yourself using delaying tactics, then re-energise by reminding yourself that the right co-founder is your key to winning without losing. Financial success and the freedom to enjoy it may not be as good as a loving family, but they are still worth a serious effort.

DESIGN ELEMENT #7:
MAKE SURE YOU HAVE ENOUGH PEOPLE TO
PICK FROM TO BE ABLE TO RECRUIT YOUR
PERFECT CO-FOUNDERS

#8 SPOT YOUR FUTURE FRIENDS

BY MARTIN BJERGEGAARD

Who would you like to spend time with more than anyone else in the world? Who revitalises you, brings out your very best and garners your unconditional trust? Your friends and family, right?

And what is important in a start-up? Energy, trust and working together towards a common vision. It's a shame you can't choose your business colleagues from the same pool of people from which you would choose your potential friends.

The relationship with your business team must be strictly business. Sure, you can be friendly with them, but it is truly a different compartment of your life. Right? Wrong. Many of our role models have proven that choosing co-founders and partners using the same criteria you would use to choose your friends is a truly effective way of doing business.

In a start-up you are blessed with a unique opportunity. An opportunity that many would wish for: the chance to pick your co-workers. Embrace this clean slate and make the most of it. Even if you create an efficient business, you will be spending a fair deal of time with your co-founders. This time, like any other time, should be enjoyable.

Does that mean that you should recruit your co-founders from amongst your closest friends and family? Maybe not – as there is indeed much to lose if things go awry. But choose what comes the closest; your future friends. People you would enjoy spending time with even without a common work project.

The chance of having fun while working together is so much greater if you genuinely like each one of your team members. The same goes for avoiding difficult situations and disagreements that evolve into a conflict and consume valuable time and energy.

Chad and Markus from Veritas Prep are personal friends. They enjoy each other's company, share interests and feed off each other's enthusiasm. They joke around like friends, because that's exactly what they are – as we are in Rainmaking. It is easy to recognise the advantages; we email, text and call each other like teenage girls. But instead of discussing Justin Bieber's latest hair-cut we passionately discuss challenges and opportunities in our businesses as well as stories from our daily endeavours. We run together, travel together and share everything. That builds and maintains a unique level of trust between us, which is undoubt-edly the most important asset in our company.

As Stephen Covey Junior says in his bestselling book *The Speed of Trust*, 'Trust is the one thing that underpins and affects the quality of every relationship, every communication, every work project, every business venture, every effort in which we are engaged. Nothing is as fast as the speed of trust, and without trust even the most well-planned initiatives fall short.'

So spot your future friends, make them your business partners, and not only will you do better, but I can assure you that the road will be that much smoother and more enjoyable than for those unfortunate entrepreneurs who hang around co-founders and colleagues every day whom they do not truly like.

DESIGN ELEMENT #8:
CHOOSE CO-FOUNDERS YOU GENUINELY LIKE

#9 GO ALL IN

BY MARTIN BJERGEGAARD

When we ask applicants to our 3-month accelerator programme, Startupbootcamp, about their founder teams, we often get answers like this: 'It's Ben and me full time, and then Jenny's helping us part-time until we get funding, so she can quit her job.'

Jenny has, of course, her reasons: rent to be paid, a family that needs food on the table. You could say that it is indeed all very admirable, that she works for free for a start-up in her spare time … or?

When not everyone in a group of founders has fully taken the leap, the team is weakened. For some, the project is 'life or death'; while for others it is an interesting side project that can be shut down with relatively few costs other than some wasted evening hours. This unevenness can of course be recognised through different equity shares, but that doesn't make the team more close-knit or effective. As long as there remains someone who hasn't gone 'all in', a good balance will probably not be achieved for anyone.

There is a reason why Jenny has been asked to be a co-founder. She has skills that are central to the new company. But as long as she's only in during evenings and weekends, these skills will only be seen as a shadow of what they could have been were she

sitting side by side with her co-founders in the most productive hours of the day.

Even more important than missing key hours is the mental gap this situation creates between team members. A start-up is difficult to pull off on a part-time basis; and next to impossible with only a partial mental commitment.

Compromises can of course be necessary. But they must be limited as much as possible. When we started Rainmaking, three of us committed fully from day one, while our fourth partner, Morten Bjerregaard Nielsen, needed 3 months to wrap up his law career in an agreeable way. We made a deal from the start that this was OK – but also that it was limited to these 3 months, and that the transition to full time was not conditional on anything other than time. There were no caveats about funding having to fall into place, a certain number of customers to sign up, or a product that had to be finished. Morten himself was the one who was most aware that he should take exactly the same risk as the rest of us – unconditionally.

Although the period when Morten had two jobs only lasted a few months, he managed to work himself up to a resting pulse of 92 before his farewell reception at the law firm. As a 29 year old who trained five times a week, Morten didn't think that health problems were something that concerned him. But his doctor's message was clear: you have to slow down a bit. Fortunately, his heart rate returned to its usual exemplary level the moment he downscaled from two jobs to one.

Likewise, from the beginning, it has been a key principle in our founder team not to pursue any business activities outside Rainmaking. We don't do this to hold each other back, but to ensure that we're always 100% in the same boat, sharing the same ups and downs with the same intensity, and are completely equal in our partnership.

Getting a good balance in life, as an entrepreneur, is easier than you'd think. But you have to get some very fundamental things right. Such as making sure that the founder team not only includes all the necessary skills, but is also dedicated and accessible enough for these qualities to be brought fully and consistently into play.

But what about that rent that has to be paid? Agreed, it can be difficult to pull off the transition from employee to entrepreneur. But be willing to consider 'radical' actions such as selling your house and moving to a small apartment, borrowing money from your parents (but please, only if they can afford to lose it), turning all your holidays for a year into bicycle trips, or even trading your car for 6 months of free housing. Whatever it takes to sufficiently free up your mental space to get your business off the ground.

In poker it's dangerous to go 'all in'. In entrepreneurship it's the only sensible thing to do.

> ## DESIGN ELEMENT #9:
> ## MAKE SURE YOU (AND YOUR CO-FOUNDERS) ARE ALL IN

#10 KEEP IT SIMPLE

BY JORDAN MILNE

The ball drops, which pushes a lever, spins a wheel and knocks over a domino, which then sends a winding row of hundreds of others toppling over. The final domino falls onto a scale that, when tipped, rises and flicks on a light switch. Task accomplished.

This type of sequence of events is typical of something called a Rube Goldberg machine, or the work of the UK illustrator Heath Robinson. Rube and Heath popularised vastly complicated and often comical machines that performed simple everyday tasks. While their machines and those they inspired may be an extreme example, it's true that many businesses falter because their products and services are too complicated and not what their customers want.

Have you ever wondered why you so often see a hugely successful idea and find yourself saying 'I could have thought of that'? Many feel that way about companies like eBay, Amazon, Dell, Wikipedia, Twitter. The list goes on and on. This is largely due to the fact that, at their root, these are all quite simple ideas. So why do so many enterprises go astray? How do things get so complicated? One possibility may be that we are simply trying to be too clever.

One company that fell victim to this trap was Boo.com. Boo was

a high-profile British Internet company that burst onto the scene in the late 1990s, eventually making its much-publicised launch in the autumn of 1999. An online fashion retailer, Boo was led by three Swedes; Ernst Malmsten, Kajsa Leander and Patrik Hedelin. The company steamrolled through $135 million dollars of venture capital funding only to be placed into receivership on 18 May 2000. It was liquidated a mere 18 months after its inception. Part of this demise can undoubtedly be attributed to the economic climate, but there was another important factor at play too: Boo was not simple. It was complicated.

The founders had initially planned to spend $40 million and to launch in 3 months with 30 employees. These plans quickly changed. Boo brought in all of the best experts to devise a strategy and by the time they went live they were several months late and their nimble team had skyrocketed into a staff of 400. By that time they had also used up over four times their initial investment. The site featured advanced flash technology that took several minutes to load, leaving users frustrated as fancy avatars directed their shopping experience. All of this before they had even brought in a dime. Things had gotten complex.

Now listen to a different story. In a small one-bedroom apartment in Vancouver, Canada, an unassuming 24 year old sits typing away at his computer. He is trying to learn the programming language ASP.NET. After some deliberation he decides the best way is to build a simple dating site. The site he builds is just the bare bones. No bells or whistles, only the necessities. Just enough for him to learn and for the site to be functional. The site goes live soon after it is built and users flock to it. The 24 year old puts on some simple banner ads and an affiliate programme to bring in revenue and capitalise on his new-found traffic. He makes the site largely self-sustaining and only works on it for 10–20 hours per week. He sits back and lets the money roll in, tinkering with the site only when he finds a more direct way to address an issue that has come up.

The young man's name is Markus Frind. His company: Plentyof-Fish.com. With 5.3 million unique visitors in February 2011 alone, according to Compete.com, it is the number one dating site in both Canada and the UK. The site is no slouch financially, bringing in estimated annual revenues upwards of $10 million. Perhaps most shocking is the fact that Markus has run his company singlehand-edly during most of its existence and now employs just a hand-ful of staff. Even more staggering is the fact that despite running the company largely by himself, having a site with only the bare minimum and using the simplest revenue generators around, Markus has been outperforming sites with hundreds of employ-ees and massive budgets. The company is thriving and recently penetrated pop culture by appearing in one of Lady Gaga's music videos.

How did he do this? He kept things simple. When he found a way that worked, he left it alone. Markus was merely looking to help his users in the simplest way he could. **He had discovered that simplicity was efficiency**.

A few hours down the Pacific coast, across the US border, lives a man named Craig Newmark. Eight years before PlentyofFish, a similar story unfolded. Craig hadn't lived in San Francisco very long and wanted to create a friendly, social event listing service. So he created a simple mailing list of fun events. Soon others were contributing to the list and it grew to include more categories. The list snowballed and subscribers kept joining. The people using it asked if Craig could build a website to take the place of the mailing list. Because his interest was in helping people, he gave them what they wanted: a simple site to list events, jobs and a handful of other categories. What started in a modest apartment in the Sunset district of San Francisco quickly became one of the biggest Internet phenomena in the world: Craigslist.

Craigslist now has 20 billion page views per month, according to Alexa.com, and is the 10th most popular website in the USA and 37th globally. It is present in 570 cities and in 50 countries. Although it is not officially a profit-making organisation, Craigslist revenues have also been reported to be climbing beyond $150 million. All of this with only 32 employees.

Certainly a site like this must be very advanced. The newest up-and-coming design backed by the latest technology? Far from it. Craigslist is something of an anomaly in the business world. Its minimalist website design has been left relatively unchanged since its birth and it is one of the simplest sites on the Internet.

So choose simple first. Simple works. Not only is it easier to implement, but it is often more effective. The next time you feel the urge to be clever, take up Sudoku or sign up for an evening class in philosophy, get it out of your system, and then go back to work and simply help your customers.

DESIGN ELEMENT #10:
MAKE A SIMPLE PRODUCT, A SIMPLE COMPANY
AND THINK SIMPLE THOUGHTS

A NEW MINDSET

→ 11 INSIGHTS FOR A BETTER QUALITY OF LIFE

The mind is a powerful tool. If you believe you can achieve a goal, chances are that you are right. If, on the other hand, you feel certain you cannot – well, then you are right too.

To find the dual optimum we described in the introduction of this book, we will need to get into the right frame of mind. We need to turn away from fear. Fear of missing out, fear of not being good enough. Those anxieties will do nothing but drain our energy. Instead, as we will soon elaborate, start looking for the good things, organise your life to have the most possible 'flow' experiences, and see self-discipline in a much brighter light. Believe that you can have it all: balance and success. The next 11 essays will show you how to optimise your mindset.

'If you can dream it, you can do it' – Walt Disney

#1 DON'T LIVE A DEFERRED LIFE

BY JORDAN MILNE

'I'll take her to the theatre as soon as I finish this round of fund-raising. I'll get back on my workout schedule after the application deadline next week. Things are really hectic this year, but next year it will be different. For now I'll just put my head down and grind it out. All this will pay off when we make an exit, and then I'll take the time to really enjoy life. I will take more vacations when I retire.'

Sound familiar?

Living a deferred life can mean different things to different people, but the essence of it, the real constant, is that you are foregoing things you want to do in the present. Putting them off until later.

Don't take the 'deferred life' route. Have fun along the way. The longer you put off what you really want to do, the greater the expected payoff must be. If you sacrifice all of your 20s or 30s, the payoff has to be huge. This is a dangerous and frustrating way to live your life. A deferred life builds resentment. Maybe not today, maybe not tomorrow, but eventually.

Randy Komisar is a partner at venture capital heavyweight Kleiner Perkins Caufield & Byers, a company that helped to build companies such as Amazon, Google, Intuit, Genentech and Sun. Located on the famous Sand Hill Road in Silicon Valley, KPCB is one of the most powerful venture capital funds in the world. It has also recently joined forces with Generation Investment, Al Gore's green investment fund. Countless entrepreneurs clamber for KPCB's attention daily. A chance to be backed by the best.

The way Randy put it when he spoke at Stanford is the best description I have heard regarding a deferred life:

'The concept of a deferred life is putting off what you really want to do right now because you believe what you need to do today is what's expected of you. It is not the notion of not paying your dues or not working hard to build a foundation for success. Those are two different ideas. It's important to understand that what's deferred is your sense of passion. What's deferred is your sense of excitement, your enthusiasm. The integration of what you're doing with what you care about.'

In his book *The Monk and the Riddle* Randy has condensed the classic deferred life plan into two stages. He explains: 'First do what you have to do. Then later hopefully do what you want to do. The problem with this plan is that those few that eventually get to step two often don't know by then what they really want to do.'

Randy goes on to distinguish between drive and passion: 'Passion pulls you toward something you cannot resist. Drive pushes you toward something you feel compelled or obligated to do.'

Randy tells us about his own moment of revelation. It came to him only after years of spiritual practice and self-examination. He says, 'I started to pay attention. I was succeeding by everyone's standards but my own. Each new success was short lived and ultimately unfulfilling. I looked back on my life and took note of those times where I had felt real satisfaction and passion. I realised that variety, creativity, ideas, and working with a blank canvas all mattered more to me than titles or salaries. I leapt off the elevator to the penthouse, expecting a free fall, but finding wings. I started setting my own expectations, my own standards, expressed my own values. To my surprise, it worked. I was able to integrate who I was with what I did sufficiently to move from the "Deferred Life Plan" to the "Whole Life Plan." I just wish I had had enough confidence to do it years ago.'

When Randy did take the risk he found that his passions became so intertwined with what he was doing that it no longer felt like work.

Call it what you want, 'living in the moment' or 'appreciating the journey'. But make sure you factor the question 'Will I enjoy this process?' into your decision: life is not a single bottom line with cash being the final verdict. **Your experiences are where it all begins and ends, so gather as many as you can**. It's about having both financial success and enjoying the ride. Take the time to live your life now. Deferred moments make for a deferred life. As Randy Komisar reminds us, 'The journey is the reward. There is nothing else.'

LIFE QUALITY ENHANCER #1:
DO WHAT YOU ALWAYS WANTED TO DO
RIGHT NOW

#2 LOOK FOR THE GOOD THINGS

BY JORDAN MILNE

When I was younger, my family lived close to my school. Every morning I would pack my lunch and then head out the door to start the short walk to the classroom. And every day, just as I was heading over the hill across from my house, I would look back over my shoulder and wave to my mother. For as long as I can remember my mother waited outside on the front porch until I was over that hill and waved back. My other strong memory from those mornings is what she would say to me every single day as I was leaving. She would look at me cheerfully and say: 'Look for the good things.' This sentence became so ingrained in my head that to this day I can still hear it clearly, in the same tone in which she said it so many years ago. It made such an impact that I still carry it with me everywhere I go.

In a start-up there are always things to be done. New customers to acquire, product launches to prepare, team members to manage, board members to please and fires to put out.

In such a setting it's easy to look at what can be improved. While a critical eye fuelled by a healthy dose of ambition is helpful, many fall into the trap of being perpetually displeased and never content with their state of affairs. In a start-up it is a given that things will be in a state of flux. That is the nature of the beast. It is to your benefit to get into the habit of focusing on what's good. Instead of walking around looking for 'what's wrong?' try looking for 'what's right?'

On a journey to achieve and maintain both success and happiness, adopting the attitude of looking for the good things helps on both fronts. Not only does being optimistic affect your mood, stress levels and overall happiness, but research has proven over and over that what you believe will happen actually has the power to influence your reality.

Rosenthal and Jacobson confirmed as far back as 1968 that expectations directly influence outcome, referring to this self-fulfilling phenomenon as the 'Pygmalion Effect', a term from the ancient Roman poet Ovid.

The reality of the Pygmalion Effect can be seen and utilised every day in the business world. For instance, if a bank is rumoured or expected to fail, people will take their money out and the prophecy will be fulfilled. On a more personal level, if you expect your business associates to perform to high standards, research has shown that they will generally rise to meet your expectations.

As John Steinbeck, the American writer, said, 'it is the nature of man to achieve greatness when greatness is expected of him'.

This is not to say that you can't set out to improve things. You should. But look for the good things, and you just may find more of them than you think.

Most people are in the habit of noticing when those around them make mistakes and are quick to point them out. As Kenneth Blanchard and Spencer Johnson teach us in their international bestseller *The One Minute Manager*, you can turn this tendency around and try *'catching someone doing something right'*. When you have done so, recognise them for it. This approach, while counter-intuitive, can boost both your efficiency and your happiness (and everyone else's).

LIFE QUALITY ENHANCER #2: NOTICE AND APPRECIATE ALL THAT WENT WELL TODAY

#3 HAVE A CHILD – OR PRETEND YOU DO

BY JORDAN MILNE

We mentioned Caterina Fake and Flick'r in an earlier essay, but let's have a closer look. Launched in 2004, Flick'r enables millions of users to organise and share their photographs and videos. Caterina and her co-founder Stewart Butterfield led the site to great success and, as of September 2010, Flick'r was hosting billions of images from users all over the world. As Flick'r quickly became an online sensation, Yahoo came calling and offered to buy the site. Yahoo's efforts ultimately paid off, with Caterina and Stewart selling the company in March of 2005. The pair had done what many only dream of: sold their company for a huge sum just 13 months after launching. Caterina went on to be named one of the '100 most influential people' by *Time* magazine as well as gracing the cover of *Newsweek*.

Caterina's success as an entrepreneur is unquestioned, but money is not her primary motivation. She recognises the true value of work–life balance, a balance that hasn't always occurred in her previous endeavours. Chris Dixon, her partner on her new venture, has had similar experiences.

'In our first start-ups we spent a lot of time "freaking out" and were not smart with our use of time. If we were working better I'd say we could have accomplished the same amount in 45 hours per week as we did in 60–70 hours per week. In my experience this is true for most folks,' says Caterina.

Balance is a priority for Caterina, and she believes she has found her own formula.

'I am trying to apply the lessons I learned building Flick'r to my new ventures. This is motivated largely by necessity. I now have a 3-year-old daughter, which is a game changer. My work time can no longer expand indefinitely, which used to be the case. But somehow I manage to get the same amount of work done anyway.'

Most parents make their kids a priority. If you have kids, put them at the top of your list. If you don't have kids, pretend you do. In other words, give all the other important things in your life (the things you depend on for your balance) the same attention you would give them if they were your children. Defend your time with them as if you were a parent.

For example: you love playing ping-pong and feel that it is important to your sense of balance, but don't have enough time in your day to practice? Make it your kid. And most of all, never be ashamed of your 'kid'. Don't sheepishly say you are sneaking off to do more work or have a 'family emergency'. Proudly proclaim what you are heading off to do and let the world hear you ping and pong.

It takes courage to stand up to convention, but gradually your critics will become your followers as they witness how playing ping-pong actually makes you both happier and more productive.

Instead of just having balance as a vague goal, make it part of your schedule and give it the attention it deserves. When you have children, you need to head home to take care of them. Treat your balance with the same dedication you would a child. Don't feel bad about saying you have to meet some friends for dinner. You do. Doing so is what keeps you at your peak performance.

LIFE QUALITY ENHANCER #3: STICK UP FOR YOUR BALANCE

#4 LEARN FROM EVERYTHING YOU DO

BY MARTIN BJERGEGAARD

In 2004, Zhang Xiangdong and two of his friends from college had a vision. They believed that in the future people would be able to get any information they needed free on their mobile phones. For that to happen, content was needed – as were some easy-to-use mobile web platforms and applications for simple tasks like checking the weather, setting up a customised screen, keeping track of your contacts, and communicating via text messages.

Fast forward to 2012 and Zhang's company 3G Portal is running the leading mobile Internet portal in China, and has seen more than 200 million downloads of its apps globally. Not a bad achievement for someone who began just 8 years ago with nothing more than a vision.

For Mr Zhang, mobile Internet is not only his job, but also his passion and a cherished hobby. However, there is much more to Mr Zhang than bits and bytes. He is a voracious reader and spends a full hour each day, and most of his Saturdays, absorbed in all kinds of literature. He has already written two books and translated another into Chinese, and now has a plan to write a drama manuscript. 'I would like to illustrate my confusion through an onstage drama,' he tells me during the interview. I ask what confuses him, and a sincere grin spreads across his face as he answers: 'The big questions in life. Like, where we come from. I think most people have a sense of confusion when they think deeply about that.'

Another hobby of the 35-year-old Beijing-based businessman is bicycling. Zhang has spent countless weeks on the roads of China, France, South Africa and Australia, and now has the goal of cycling across five continents. Each of his weekdays starts off with one hour on the bike, from 8 am to 9 am. So what motivates him to spend so much time in the saddle? 'It's part of human nature. I believe life should have diversity. We must all make sure to have fun while pursuing our ambitions,' he explains. He then shares with me a Chinese saying that is not easily translated, but goes something like this: 'Happiness is natural in life, however most often we realise it too late.' I find myself nodding in agreement.

As if his genuine dedication to literature, bicycling and business wasn't enough, Mr Zhang has also taken the initiative in creating an ambitious and far-reaching cultural project. Under the umbrella name Meridian, a handful of visionary endeavours have been laid out. Each activity has the purpose of unleashing and unifying creative potential across time zones, borders and cultures. One project is to collect fairytales for children from multiple countries, and then make localised versions of them, starting with the Chinese audience. Another project is to interview taxi drivers in 12 of the fastest-growing Chinese cities to reveal how urbanisation looks from the frontlines. Under the tagline 'Created in China' and with the values of being 'Curious, Creative and Global', Meridian, a non-profit, non-governmental organisation, seeks to produce 'thought-provoking collaborative works'.

Much of Zhang's inspiration, thinking and confidence can be traced back to the numerous hours spent on his bike, alone in a foreign country and culture. 'Curiosity is my driver, and each bike trip is a conversation with oneself,' Zhang explains. For instance, bicycling has taught him important lessons about how to run a company. From time to time the weather will be bad, there will be hills to climb and unforeseen difficulties. You just have to accept that. You have to be patient and persistent. Have belief and keep practising. Find your own pace and stick to it. According to Zhang, running a business is the same. When asked if his hobbies compromise his business ventures, Zhang responds, 'not at all'. In fact, he feels they make him a better leader, innovator and businessman.

Many of us believe that time spent on private hobbies does nothing to add value to our business or career. Zhang Xiangdong shows us that this doesn't need to be the case. If we enter each activity with an open mind, we will be amazed by how much relevant learning can be gained from seemingly unrelated pursuits.

How many parents have improved their collaboration and leadership skills through interacting with their children? How often has reading a book offered fresh perspectives that could be used to tackle a business problem? What about travelling to faraway places, being dedicated to a sport, unfolding your potential as an at-home chef or an amateur photographer?

It might not be obvious at the time, but the truth is that a holistic life containing different experiences sharpens our business skills, not the opposite. To learn from everything we do is a viable strategy for success, and Mr Zhang shows us one possible application of that insight. He concludes the interview by stating: 'Everyone is their own master. We should each pick our own way of life.' Fortunately for us, this means that we should feel no pressure to follow his lead in doing 100 push-ups each morning.

LIFE QUALITY ENHANCER #4:
LIVE LIFE AND GET A NEW PERSPECTIVE

#5 FEEL THE FLOW AT HOME

BY MARTIN BJERGEGAARD

Let's be honest: when we are really passionate about a project at work, many of us find it easier to engage ourselves in that than in our domestic and spare-time activities. It gives us more energy to plan the product launch than to change a nappy. It's easier to stay present at the investor meeting than during dinner. Your child experiences a less enthusiastic version of you than your customers do. If we don't watch out, this can be a serious pitfall for those of us who love our work. The role models we interviewed for this book were all very conscious of this challenge. For them, it's not enough to be fully present in one part of their life. They strive for awareness and enjoyment in all areas of life.

Henning Daverne, who we mentioned in an earlier essay, has a strategy for how to succeed at this. It's about flow. Flow is when time and space cease to exist, when you're 100% focused on what is right in front of you, when you don't want to go somewhere else or think of anything else. Flow is a fantastic state to be in. Typically there are three preconditions that enable us to get into a state of flow:

- The task is meaningful to us;
- Our skills are in good balance with the challenge of the problem to be solved;

- There are clear goals and an immediate satisfaction in completing the task.

In recent years we've become better at creating frameworks to experience flow at work. This is especially true for entrepreneurs, as we have chosen our own mission and the people with whom we accomplish it. But what about in our personal lives?

Within a family it is often tough to agree on what you all want to do. Your child wants to play and you want to cook. The challenge of the activity is often hard to spot. Playing with Barbie dolls might seem dull to you and, to your child's dissatisfaction, your thoughts drift towards your inbox. There is another way. Try to think of one of those days when you moved, took care of the entire garden, painted the house, planned your holiday, built a playhouse, made a complete town out of Lego or hosted a barbecue for all of your neighbours.

Think of a time when you and your family or friends were all miraculously engaged in the same endeavour, totally agreed on what the goal was, and all had roles that were challenging but possible for each of you to fulfil. It was fantastic, right? It created a shared experience that you've often talked about since, and which you all appreciate, despite the fact that it was perhaps unclear as to how or why it occurred. Now look back at those three preconditions, and see if it becomes clearer.

By incorporating flow into our personal lives, we can consciously create more fun, meaningful and life-affirming

experiences. With a little focus and a determined effort to over-come inertia, we can jump-start unique shared experiences for our families, our friends and ourselves. Do you feel, like me, that you have some friendships that have become too routine based? Make the decision that your next meeting will be built around a common flow experience. Try going on a 3-day bike ride, fishing, walking 100 km in a weekend, or perhaps learning to kayak.

If we only really enjoy our work, we may easily get stuck in it far past both our optimum efficiency and optimum happiness. By making our spare time just as rewarding as our work hours, we automatically avoid falling into that trap.

> # LIFE QUALITY ENHANCER #5:
> # CREATE FLOW BY MAKING SHARED GOALS AND
> # CHALLENGES IN YOUR PRIVATE LIFE

#6 GIVE BACK, GET PERSPECTIVE

BY JORDAN MILNE

In the spring of 2009 a dinner was held in New York City, initiated by the two wealthiest men in America – Bill Gates and Warren Buffett – and hosted by David Rockefeller Sr. The guest list was short, but everyone in attendance had one thing in common: they were all billionaires. In the year that followed, a series of exclusive dinners was held at various locations across the United States, all of them with Bill Gates and Warren Buffett as hosts. Guests included heavyweights from business, politics and entertainment such as Baron Hilton, Oprah Winfrey, Michael Bloomberg, Ted Turner, George Lucas, Mark Zuckerberg and Jim Simons (touted as 'The World's Smartest Billionaire' by the *Financial Times*). And the guest list was just the tip of the iceberg.

What went on behind closed doors was subject to much speculation. Was a new world order being established? What could people with this much power, influence and wealth be plotting?

What eventually emerged, however, was something quite unexpected. These billionaires were indeed devising a plan. The plan, however, was not for global domination, but for the most effective way to give away their money to charity and the best method for convincing others to do the same.

The plan was an organised initiative spawned by Gates and Buffett to encourage the world's billionaires, starting with the Americans on the Forbes 400 list, to pledge most of their wealth to philanthropic causes. The initiative that would change the world of philanthropy for ever would come to be known as 'The Giving Pledge'. To date 69 billionaires have signed up. All Americans. Next up: China and India.

All those in the pledge have made their money in different ways and have led quite different lives. Although they have varying reasons for giving away their wealth, what they share is the passion to give. They know that giving is a win–win scenario. Good for the recipients, but also good for the giver.

Recent neuropsychological research reviewed by the University of Notre Dame in Indiana shows that donating to charity activates neural areas of the brain that are linked to reward processing; the same areas that are activated by pleasures such as eating and sex. Studies suggest that even small donations spark these pleasurable psychological experiences. Giving your time counts too. This research gives a physical basis to the long-running behavioural study conducted by Paul Wink and Michele Dillon. Starting in the 1930s they followed a group of California residents and found that those who engaged in giving stayed both healthier and happier as they got older. **You may not be a billionaire, but it is never too early or too late to enjoy the benefits of giving. Giving your time counts too.**

It is surprisingly easy to get to a point where we think the world revolves around our business and us. Focusing on our ventures is an important part of the equation for success, but keeping our lives in perspective is critical to our own life balance. We need to see our projects in the greater context of our lives and the global community, as well as in relation to those who are less fortunate.

So if we want to learn from these billionaires and scientists, live a longer, happier life and have as much fun as eating a gourmet meal or rolling around in bed (well, almost), then we should try reaching into our pockets and giving a bit more often.

LIFE QUALITY ENHANCER #6:
MAKE A GIFT OR A DONATION EVERY WEEK

#7 RETHINK SELF-DISCIPLINE

BY MARTIN BJERGEGAARD

Many of us think of self-discipline as getting something done that we really don't want to do. For an entrepreneur, this could be doing our taxes, canvassing to get new customers or updating our cash flow budget. These types of duties are ones we often postpone and procrastinate about.

Traditionally, the attitude has been that successful entrepreneurs enjoy success in part because they are self-disciplined enough to complete these less desirable tasks. Our conversations with our role models, however, suggested another track: what if it is the other way around? What if what actually creates success in business is the ability to spend the maximum amount of time on what you really enjoy doing? For some people this may mean representing the company to customers, for others developing the world's best software and for others still it might be about leading and inspiring a team.

Some call it flow, others call it energy, focus or presence, but whatever word we use, the meaning is the same: to let ourselves be completely absorbed in what we are doing. When time and space are suspended and we are at one with our actions we can be 3, 5 or even 10 times as productive as when we exercise 'self-discipline' and force ourselves to stray from the things we really want to be doing.

There is nothing wrong with pleasure. It is no less honourable doing what you enjoy than fighting your way through a tax return. That being said, a lot of people love doing accounting and don't exactly love doing the very things that may excite *you*.

We all know that specialisation works and, just because we are entrepreneurs, it doesn't mean that that fundamental principle no longer applies. We can easily outsource assignments to others. We don't have to do it all by ourselves. A great many things can be outsourced or delegated today, so the challenge becomes to find the core of what makes our pulse rise and our blood flow so that we can be pulled into that 100%, and then let ourselves do it.

Most of us can answer the question of what we don't feel like doing. It is more difficult to get a grip on what we really *want* to do. In other words, what we would do even if we didn't get paid to do it, and even if no one else believed in us: the core of our motivation, our true passion.

Self-discipline is still important, it just means something new: it means to 'force' ourselves to spend as much time as possible doing what we love. If we succeed in this task, everything follows naturally. We will easily get someone to do the tasks we don't enjoy, our customers will find their way to us and our projects will act like a magnet in attracting talented colleagues.

We recognise flow, energy and presence when we see it. All too often, however, we let ourselves get distracted by the common misconception that everything has to hurt a little. We feel that we have to force ourselves to do things we don't really want to do. There is something appealing about playing the role of the martyr, but it is not the way to the good life. Use your self-discipline to speed yourself up, not slow yourself down.

'Choose a job you love, and you will never have to work a day in your life' – Confucius

LIFE QUALITY ENHANCER #7: USE YOUR SELF-DISCIPLINE TO FOCUS ON THE TASKS YOU ARE PASSIONATE ABOUT

#8 GET YOUR TEAM BALANCED

BY JORDAN MILNE

Two months ago, after a series of impulse flights, bus rides and motorcycle adventures, I found myself travelling in Laos, South-East Asia. In addition to being in one of the most beautiful countries I have ever visited, the small town of Luang Prebang, which became our home for the week, also played host to one of the most elaborate night markets one could imagine. A veritable circus of organised chaos touched every sense, as stalls showcasing brightly coloured goods lined the streets as far as the eye could see. All topped off with the curious smells of freshly made local cuisine floating in the air.

The market was lively and vibrant, with passers-by walking among the stalls and bargaining with local merchants for their hand-crafted goods. I eventually spotted something I liked enough to enter into the process I had witnessed so many others engaged in. The bargaining went back and forth. Both of us starting miles apart, knowing full well that we were out of line and would soon meet near the middle. It was like a dance. After several numbers, the vendor looked up and, as we settled on the magic one, she spoke the following words with a mischievous look in her eye: 'Good deal for me. Good deal for you.' I laughed, as I had heard that phrase several times in the 10 minutes leading up to this point, but I accepted. 'Good deal for me. Good deal for you,' I repeated with a smile. The same phrase can also be applied to balance.

When we think about balance, we most often think about it for ourselves. Team balance, however, is just as important if we want to enjoy and get the most out of our personal balance. What is good for you is also good for your team. And vice versa. Some companies have a culture that hinders balance. Some team members lead exciting and balanced lives, while others work constantly and are incredibly imbalanced. This inequality is dangerous and builds resentment from both sides:

-   Those who aren't able to do something fun because they are completely immersed in work resent those who do have that opportunity. They get jealous and feel that they are carrying the whole workload (whether rightfully or not).

-   Those who live a balanced life and do enjoy their evenings resent the others because they feel they have to hide it and downplay the enjoyment they get from their experiences.

Resentment leads to bad feelings and hurt relationships, which ultimately stifles productivity.

The most effective entrepreneurs we interviewed recognised that being balanced helped them to become better and more fulfilled leaders. But they also recognised that they could only have productive teams if that balance, and the opportunity to lead incredible, satisfying lives, was afforded to everyone. Companies where employees all do fun and exciting things and return to work to share those experiences with their team members create a special bond and a far more compassionate culture than companies that don't. By caring more about who you work with, you also become more inspired and work more intensely for each other. Team loyalty produces more effective results.

So, help and encourage your team to achieve balance. Talk about experiences outside work and seek out team members who share your love and need for this liberating lifestyle. Doing so will not only allow you to enjoy it more but will make them happier and more productive, in turn making your business more efficient. Good deal for you, good deal for them.

LIFE QUALITY ENHANCER #8:
MAKE SURE YOUR WHOLE TEAM HAS
THE OPPORTUNITY FOR BALANCE

#9 YOU ARE NOT YOUR WORK

BY JORDAN MILNE

Many of us are so attached to our business that it defines our identity. This identification is often so strong that our personal ups and downs are tied directly to the ups and downs of our company. When our business is going well, we are relatively carefree. When we hit troubled waters, well, that's another story. This is a dangerous way to work and live.

By living this way, not only are we narrowing our experiences, but we are making success harder to achieve and maintain. Instead we should also find happiness outside work and have our sense of self be tied to more than one thing. Keep things in perspective. **Many of us believe that we will be happy and confident after becoming successful in our business life. The reality is that the confidence and positive attitude are not things that come after our success, but qualities that when developed will in turn enable us to succeed.**

Jake Nickell, founder of Threadless, not only knows this reality but lives it. Jake came from humble beginnings. When he was in his early 20s he could barely pay the rent on his $400 per month apartment. Jake did, however, possess something far more valuable than money. He had a distinct sense of self-worth, unconnected to his level of outward success, and he created this sense of self-esteem in two ways. First, he had close relationships with friends and family. At the same time he developed a clear picture both of the kind of person he wanted to be and of his desire to exert a positive influence on the world around him.

'It's all about relationships and how you want to impact the world. Not just as a big idea but walking down the street – the kind of guy you want to be,' Jake says.

His sense of self-worth made him happy. It also made him feel confident. This same confidence gave him the courage to go out on a limb and start his company, and eventually to achieve great success.

'Starting out, I had a lot of self-confidence and very little fear about learning new things. I started the company one hour after I came up with the idea. I only had $500, was still in college and had never printed a T-shirt before in my life. We just said "let's ask people to design their own shirts". And they did! We held our first T-shirt competition on an online forum, without even having our own website. Five days later we figured out which ones we were going to print. At that point we didn't even know how we were going to print them. Our confidence allowed us to jump in and figure it out as we went along.'

Not only did his independent sense of worth give Jake the confidence to take the leap and start a company, it also made him better equipped to weather the inherent rollercoaster ride that business brings with it. Being less vulnerable to that up and down means he can make more clear-headed decisions. Jake has now been successfully running Threadless for 10 years and dodging most of the curve balls the business has thrown his way.

Thanks to Threadless, Jake is now a multimillionaire, but he still insists that he was just as happy when he was living in his $400 apartment.

Your 'outside-of-work' identity can come from many places. It could start with something as simple as joining a sports team.

John Vechey is the co-founder of video game maker and publisher PopCap Games. He and his co-founders started the company in Seattle in the year 2000 and have grown it to over 600 employees. John is now one of the most successful young entrepreneurs in the world. He too emphasises the importance of having an independent sense of self-worth:

'Several years ago was a very stressful time for me while building my company. At that very same time I decided to join a sports team for fun. This decision turned out to be critical in that it gave me a sense of identity and a team outside of PopCaps. When things were rough at work, my sense of who I am wasn't shaken because I had something that I could balance it out with. I was using that to get through a hard time.

'In my opinion everyone should have something else while they're starting companies, whether that is cooking, a sport, exercise or family. Balance is key.' Today, at 32 years of age, John Vechey has just sold his business in a billion-dollar deal.

Spiritual teachers, from Buddha in India in the 6th century BC to Eckhart Tolle in Canada in the year 2011, profess that everything we need to feel complete and happy already exists within ourselves. We don't need a successful company, fame or fortune to be happy. Start being happy right now and then build those externalities just for the fun of it.

Work will form a portion of your identity, but to have a better shot at success and sustainable happiness, take a page from Jake and John: add other ingredients into the mix that make up your whole self.

> ## LIFE QUALITY ENHANCER #9:
> ## FIND YOUR SENSE OF SELF-WORTH FROM MORE SOURCES THAN JUST YOUR BUSINESS

#10 DON'T BE AFRAID OF MISSING OUT

BY JORDAN MILNE

Earlier we mentioned that Sophie Vandebroek is an advocate of streamlining her relationships. That might seem counter-intuitive when our goal is to live a life full of happiness and success. So let's take a closer look.

'I just keep a handful of close friends and this frees up lots of time,' says Sophie. This extra time she uses to take care of herself, relax and spend time with family and those close friends. Keeping a small number of friends is not anti-social behaviour. Sophie is a compassionate, loving and social person. Her practice instead speaks of her prioritisation of quality over quantity. She does not fall victim to the pressures that so many of us do of thinking we should have hundreds of 'friends'.

We all know that person on Facebook who boasts of having a couple of thousand friends. They may have won some bragging rights, but I would be willing to bet the farm that they would be hard pressed to rattle off the names of one tenth of their list. I must admit to being guilty of this myself, feeling a strange, collector's sense of satisfaction when my number of Facebook friends ticked past the 500 mark. And who was my 500th friend? The girlfriend of the brother-in-law of a guy my sister went to school with (I think). Yes, we're very close.

Not to say that our Facebook activity is necessarily a reflection of our approach to everything else, let alone our values, but it is certainly indicative of a widespread trend. And the backlash has begun. Take talk show host Jimmy Kimmel, who declared November the 17th as 'National UnFriend Day' in the USA in an effort to defend friendship as something sacred. Fast food giant Burger King even based a promotional campaign around unfriending people on Facebook. In exchange for unfriending 10 'friends' you receive a free Whopper burger.

We are not, however, advocating getting rid of genuine friends or even having fewer friends just for the sake of it. Cultivating your network is important for growth, especially for entrepreneurs. Being exposed to new people opens up novel information pathways, which can lead to fresh ideas and partnerships. In fact, as humans our relationships are absolutely one of the most important and enjoyable parts of our lives. But that doesn't mean we have to buy into the idea that more is better.

This pressure often manifests itself as FOMO (or Fear Of Missing Out), the anxiety and stress that people experience when they suspect they are missing out on something their friends are (or may be) doing.

The truth is that no one can experience everything, and everyone on this planet is missing out on something all of the time. The real winners are the people who get this, and make it their life purpose to become the centre of their own experience, to be the life and soul of their own 'party'.

In a life where time is of the essence, look around and take a moment to become aware of the dangers of this contemporary obsession with numbers. Reflect on your own relationships, those that are truly valuable to your life, happiness, success and energy. Value can mean many things, not just in terms of what you can get from your friends, but also what you can give.

Take the time to be the kind of friend you would like to have instead of only being a friend on paper. As Sophie does, focus on quality. Not only will your relationships be more fulfilling but you will also have more time to do what YOU choose.

LIFE QUALITY ENHANCER #10:
FOCUS FIRST ON YOUR
MOST IMPORTANT FRIENDS

#11 FIND YOUR OXYGEN MASK

BY JORDAN MILNE

'Today we will be cruising at an altitude of 32,000 feet. Please make sure your luggage is stored safely in the overhead bins.' While sitting in the middle seat, jockeying subtly for the much-coveted elbow room on an Air Canada flight from London to Toronto, I heard the flight attendant begin to run through the usual safety routine:

'In the case of an emergency the oxygen masks will drop from the overhead compartment in front of you. If travelling with a child, please make sure to secure your own mask before assisting them and others.'

These were words I had heard many times before, but today, for some unknown reason, they sounded different. Today they had new meaning.

The instruction is simple enough. Yet in a panicked situation you can bet that many smart, well-intentioned people would neglect it. When instincts kick in they would help their child first. In the heat of the moment many would forget to help themselves and thus put the child at risk.

The instruction and the lesson it implies are clear, and they ring just as true in business, and in life in general, as in the confines of a 747. Just as you are better prepared to help your child if you are wearing your oxygen mask and not gasping for air, so too are you more capable of helping your business and those around you if you have taken care of yourself first.

Too many entrepreneurs burn the candle at both ends, work relentlessly and as a consequence neglect themselves. They let self-care slip and fall by the wayside, tumbling down the priority list until it is ultimately booted off altogether.

How many times have you skipped breakfast so you can keep up with your inbox, foregone basketball with your friends to finish up at the office or missed out on seeing your kid in a play because your meeting went late?

Common wisdom tells us that we must push our limits and work non-stop in order to get ahead. This attitude implies that we can work at full efficiency for an unlimited amount of time. We can't. Henry Ford knew this in 1914 when he made an announcement that sent shock waves through the business community: he called for a reduced work week in his industry.

Today, even in longstanding professions like medicine, people are finally starting to question assumptions as arguments are made to limit the work hours of junior doctors. The airline industry is following suit. In 2010, the European Union stated its intent to limit the number of hours that pilots are allowed to work daily, based on the finding that fatigue causes up to a fifth of all fatal air crashes worldwide.

We all know that taking care of ourselves is important, but taking care of ourselves first is the *real* key. This strategy is not selfish. Doing so simply enables us to function at peak efficiency when building our business, our lives and our ability to serve others.

If we fail to put on our own oxygen mask first, we are incapable of focusing on the task at hand, are preoccupied in meetings and, when pushed, are irritable to customers, colleagues, friends and family. Even something as simple as finding a matching sock can seem like an insurmountable task. Not only does neglecting ourselves make our own lives unpleasant, it is also detrimental for our business and ultimately for those around us.

With your own 'oxygen mask' on, you are definitely better equipped to deal with intangibles such as creativity and split-second decision-making.

We know it is dangerous to make decisions when we are not at our best. Even so, we often go in to work tired or hungry and think we can tackle big challenges. In many circles, pushing on in this self-sacrificing manner is seen as admirable. In reality, however, work done in this state is highly ineffective, even dangerous. So why accept it? Next time you are strung out and faced with an important decision, try taking an attitude of: 'This is a really important decision, so I'm going for a nap and then I'll make it.' Or when faced with overload when you are not at your best, take 30 minutes for a walk around the block. People may consider you crazy, but they will change their minds when they see that you end up making better decisions and delivering results.

So what is your oxygen mask? What must you do to stay feeling good and working efficiently?

Maybe it's something relatively conventional like exercise or a nap. During the Second World War, Winston Churchill would nap for about an hour in the early afternoon. As he wrote in *The Gathering Storm*, the first volume of his memoirs, 'Nature had not intended mankind to work from eight in the morning until midnight without the refreshment of blessed oblivion which, even if it only lasts 20 minutes, is sufficient to renew all the vital forces.'

Your oxygen mask may be something totally unique to you.

Many successful entrepreneurs have discovered their own individual oxygen masks – that particular thing that nourishes their body and spirit and sets them up to move on to the next task. It could be something that focuses and calms, or alternatively that excites and gets their adrenalin pumping. It could even be taking two baths a day, like the aforementioned Jake Nickell of Threadless.com.

Find your oxygen mask. And put it on first. Do this every day. And then go out and conquer the world.

LIFE QUALITY ENHANCER #11:
TAKE CARE OF YOURSELF FIRST

TAKE ACTION

→ 6 STEPS TO TAKE THIS WEEK

We have talked a lot about taking action as a way of building momentum in our entrepreneurial endeavours. The same principle applies if you choose to implement some of the strategies in this book. Chances are that you will either try this out during the coming week, or it will never happen at all. So how about taking some small steps right now? In this final chapter we outline 6 simple actions you can take to immediately start creating the life and business you want.

START NOW.

#1 TRY AN HOUR OF FULL EFFICIENCY

BY JORDAN MILNE

One hour can be used a million ways, from mindlessly skimming blogs to making a deal that will catapult your business forward for years. Not all hours are created equal.

Try this: only work one hour tomorrow. It could be 6 am to 7 am or 8 pm to 9 pm. The time of day doesn't matter. You might have a favourite time. I like sunrise. All that matters is that you only work a single hour. **By setting yourself a very limited amount of work time you are forced to be extremely focused and as efficient as possible**. So try to accomplish as much as you can in that single hour. Tomorrow.

Then look back at how you spent your time. How much did you get done? What did you do differently? For the best insight try this exercise once a week for 4 weeks. Experiment with different approaches each week, such as varying the time of day, changing location or using a different method of preparation. Once you have identified your ideal working strategies you can seek to replicate them more and more often in your normal working day.

Imagine how much you could achieve by working for 6–8 hours at peak performance every day.

EXERCISE #1:
WORK ONE HOUR, AND JUST ONE HOUR, AT FULL INTENSITY

#2 DON'T STAND IN LINE

BY JORDAN MILNE

In a time when many careers involve sitting down in front of a computer all day, physical activity on the job is not the norm – and our bodies are feeling the negative effects. Studies have shown that even if we take the recommended amount of exercise, leading a mainly sedentary lifestyle can have drastic effects on our health and mood.

In the light of this, we examined the lifestyles of each of our role models. Most of them agreed that physical activity should not be restricted to the gym, and many had found a way to intersperse their day with moments of physical activity.

Find your own opportunities, take advantage of them and build them into your routine. Take the stairs instead of the lift, and save some time on the Stairmaster. Once you start looking, you will begin to find these tricks everywhere. Watching TV at home? Do push-ups during the commercials. Sitting all day at your desk? Use a Bosu ball as a desk chair. Do isometrics while reading or talking on the phone.

Building these activities into your overall lifestyle not only gives you the momentary buzz of extra oxygen and endorphin release, but also the long-term benefits of a healthier body, which affects confidence, happiness and effectiveness both at work and at home.

Next time you see a group of people waiting impatiently for the lift, refuse to join the crowd and stand in line. Instead simply smile, and take the stairs.

EXERCISE #2:
SEIZE THE NEXT CHANCE YOU GET FOR AN OPPORTUNISTIC MINI-WORKOUT

#3 DO THE WORST FIRST

BY JORDAN MILNE

We all know the feeling. We think about it all night: we get to work and procrastinate all morning. Olin Miller, author, was onto something when he said: 'If you want to make an easy job seem mighty hard, just keep putting off doing it.'

The task could be anything: contacting a difficult customer or supplier, getting a new IP phone system installed, or working on a revised marketing strategy.

Most of us have a task or two on our list that we dread. Putting these tasks off feeds a distraction and anxiety that saps our energy. Often, actually doing the task would take just 10 minutes of our time, but we turn that into 3 hours of wasted energy fretting about doing it instead.

When you wake up tomorrow and make your to-do list for the day try to identify which is the task you find the most difficult. Most often you will know the hardest job before you even write it down – it may even give you a negative physical reaction just thinking about it. **Once you have identified this task, put it straight to the top of your list. Do the 'worst' first**.

Of course, in the longer term you should get rid of tasks that don't

excite you, so that you can focus on the missions that truly energise you. But in the meantime, and when necessary, it can be a good habit to get annoying duties over and done with, instead of letting them hang over your head.

Dale Carnegie put it this way: 'Do the hard jobs first. The easy jobs will take care of themselves.'

EXERCISE #3:
START TOMORROW BY DOING
THE THING THAT HAS BEEN HANGING
OVER YOUR HEAD ALL WEEK

#4 PUSH FOR PURPOSE

BY MARTIN BJERGEGAARD

Is it good to be hungry? For an entrepreneur most people would probably say yes. But that is to view things from the perspective of performance alone, and does not take your personal happiness into account.

Hunger is not happiness; hunger is hunger. And as long as you're hungry you'll look tirelessly for ways to become satisfied. The problem for us entrepreneurs is that one success alone is never enough to satisfy us. Our eyes are immediately fixed on the next hill – and the hunger will start growing in our stomachs again.

Many believe that the alternative to a thirst for challenges is laziness. And in many cases that is true. But there is actually another dimension. A place where you're full of energy and wonderfully satisfied at the same time. That place is called 'purpose'.

Once you find your purpose in life, you no longer need to be pushed by others or even to push yourself. You won't lose courage when faced with adversity, and you won't waste time and energy comparing yourself to others. You start to experience a genuine and spontaneous happiness simply by being effective and working on your mission.

Sounds too good to be true? Unfortunately it is for most of us. But, if anything, this is due to the fact that we haven't been looking intentionally for our purpose, not because that blissful state does not exist. It is impossible to find the formula for purpose, but you know it when you see it. Once you've found it you're no longer in doubt.

Why do you do what you do? To earn money, to make your parents proud, to prove that you are good enough, or because you imagine that's what it looks like to be successful? Or because you cannot help it, because you truly and wholeheartedly love your project and the impact it has on you and others, because the birds sing and the sky opens up every time you focus on it?

Only you can measure that difference and do something about it.

As an entrepreneur it's a good start to find your own purpose, but that in itself is not enough. You are responsible for everyone else in your team finding theirs too. Tony Hsieh has done it in Zappos, and Christian Stadil has done it in Hummel: created a 'purpose environment' where the corporate identity is so strong and clear that it sucks people in with the same purpose and supports them in living it out every today. The result is exponential effectiveness and happiness at the same time.

Leaders and entrepreneurs often feel that their team members are less dedicated than they are themselves – and they're annoyed by it, and think that perhaps firmer management or tighter control is the answer to the problem. What they overlook is that they haven't done their preparatory work and now they're paying the price: they haven't created a company with a clear and exciting mission, they haven't recruited colleagues who are sincerely turned on by this particular project, and they haven't made sure that everyone understands his or her role and its contribution to the whole.

These leaders grab a hammer and thrash themselves and the system, while in fact what they need is a trip back to the drawing board. Most of us probably recognise that leader in ourselves at times – the challenge is to quickly realise when you're falling into the trap, and get back on the right course.

If you haven't already found it, then make this year the year you discover and dare to live out your true purpose – without fears or reservation. And make next year the year you ensure that everyone in your team is able to attain the same outrageously beautiful (and frighteningly productive) state.

You can start by asking yourself five questions:

1) When am I happiest?
2) Why does that specific activity make me so happy?
3) How can I create a business centred around performing the activities that I enjoy the most?
4) What is holding me back?
5) How do I conquer these challenges, and over the next 12 months create a new framework for myself that supports me in living out my purpose?

'A happy life is one which is lived in accordance with your own true nature' – Marcus Annaeus Seneca

EXERCISE #4:
SPEND 2 HOURS THINKING ABOUT
YOUR PURPOSE IN LIFE

#5 IDENTIFY YOUR ELEPHANT TRAPS

BY JORDAN MILNE

Earlier we talked about how we all tend to waste a lot of time and energy. With this new perspective still fresh in mind, it is now time to take a systematic approach to eliminating your own particular 'elephant traps'. Do so by reviewing your habitual activities – the irritating ones that absorb most of your time – and putting them in one of two buckets. **Are they true time-wasters or are they simply things you need to control?**

If they are true time-wasters then you need to bid them farewell. The first step is to acknowledge them as culprits that take up your valuable time. Next, try to estimate how much time you spend on them every day or week. Write that number down. Giving this time-waster a concrete number will help you remember it and consciously eliminate it (I think it will surprise you too). Every time you find yourself returning to this routine, the fact that you have given it a red flag as a time-waster should trigger your brain to think twice about what you are doing.

If it is not a true time-waster, but something you really need to do, then it's about controlling the time you spend on it. It falls into the second bucket. Give yourself a fixed and dedicated amount of time to do these activities. Scheduled time facilitates control. This could mean 30 minutes at a certain time of day to write your emails or 15 minutes to place phone calls after you have accomplished a certain task.

By recognising that these are activities that will be part of your day, and giving them a start and end time, you will be less likely to sneak them in or use them as procrastination tools. Simply enjoy them for what they are (guilt free) and do them for the given time you have put aside. When the time is done, stop. Once a month, re-evaluate how you spend your time and look out for your elephant traps. As your schedule, skills, priorities and projects change, so too do your time-wasters. By setting aside a period of self-reflection every month you can stay on top of what your current traps are – helping you to keep one step ahead of the game.

EXERCISE #5:
WRITE DOWN WHAT YOU WASTE YOUR PRECIOUS TIME DOING THAT DOESN'T SIGNIFICANTLY ADD TO EITHER YOUR PERFORMANCE OR YOUR HAPPINESS

#6 TAKE TOMORROW OFF

BY JORDAN MILNE

You are probably very, very busy. Maybe you are even starting to feel a little overwhelmed, stressed out, or just not enjoying life as much as you would like to. What to do? How can you get off this treadmill of contrived urgency? Take tomorrow off. That's right. Tomorrow. This may seem impossible to you because you simply have so much to do. Maybe you could take a day off in a few weeks, or in a month, if you really planned for it – but surely not tomorrow.

And that is exactly the point. **Taking tomorrow off is an exercise in realising that most things aren't as pressing as we think and that a little time away from the office isn't the end of the world.** By taking this seemingly impossible leap of faith you will gain a new sense of freedom, perspective and energy that will help both your business and yourself.

So what should you do on this day off? The answer is whatever will give you energy. Go to the beach, play with your kids, watch an entire season of *The Sopranos* in one go or take a full day's hike in the wilderness. Take the day to rejuvenate yourself. It may just end up being the most efficient day of your year.

The day off will:

- Remind you that you are in control of your own life (who knows what revisiting that insight might lead to?);

- Boost your creativity; no one gets their best ideas with a full to-do list in their head;

- Stimulate you physically, especially if you use the opportunity to try out something new. Have you ever tried wakeboarding, making your own sushi or doing yoga?;

- Give you a healthy sense of separation from your business, helping to build stronger self-esteem.

Do that and chances are you will feel enthusiastic, clear-sighted, grounded and reconnected to your vision. Not a bad place to start if you're looking for efficiency.

So channel the excitement you got when you were a kid and had a holiday. Tomorrow, the day is all yours …

EXERCISE #6:
CONGRATULATIONS,
YOU'VE FINISHED THE BOOK — NOW TAKE
A DAY OFF TO CELEBRATE, DIGEST AND
REJUVENATE!

THE 66 STRATEGIES IN FULL – TO GET YOU WINNING WITHOUT LOSING TODAY

EFFICIENCY BOOSTERS

#1   Gather a team of great co-founders

#2   Don't sit around and wait. Get out there and start something

#3   Pick a timely project

#4   Make it a habit to test everything on a small scale

#5   Put yourself in a high-energy, inspiring environment with other entrepreneurs

#6   Always look for ways to stand out

#7   Allow the new IT tools and technologies to do some of your work for you

#8   Make sure you spend enough time with your team

#9   Hook up with people who share your passion

#10   Listen intently to honestly understand the other's perspective

#11   Apply the Lean approach to your daily activities

#12   Relax and enjoy the process

#13   Dare to follow your energy

#14   Meditate for 12 minutes a day

#15   Make being fully rested a key priority

NEW WAYS OF DOING OLD THINGS

#16   Take walking, running or biking meetings

#17   Turn your To Do list into a Today list

#18   Build your own circle of knowledge

#19   Consciously insert mind-freeing moments throughout
      your day

#20   Don't try to get everything done, just the few things that
      really matter

TIME SAVERS

#21   Choose the right project

#22   Avoid people who drain your energy

#23   If you have to get from A to B, be smart about it

#24   Deal with conflicts in person

#25   Don't delay tough decisions

#26   Clear your agenda of activities that don't add value to your
      life

#27   Don't let the details keep you from seeing the big picture

#28   Don't deal with, or be, an asshole

#29 Relax and let others contribute

#30 Get to the point

#31 Take every opportunity to get people excited about your project

#32 Be smart about raising money

#33 Don't be a slave to your emails

#34 Avoid unnecessary conflicts

EMPOWERING THOUGHTS FOR TOUGH TIMES

#35 Trouble = challenges = growth = happiness

#36 Each setback is a new opportunity

#37 Regardless of your current situation, winning without losing is possible for you

#38 It is all about making many attempts (and persevering on the right ones)

#39 People older (and younger) than you are starting up their first business today

DESIGN ELEMENTS FOR A BALANCED LIFE

#40 Pick a business that's suitable for balance

#41 Figure out how to acquire the skills to be prepared for your next venture

#42 Split up and protect your day, don't let work take it all over

#43 Think ahead to secure your future balance

#44 Always have access to fresh air

#45 Live somewhere that excites you

#46 Make sure you have enough people to pick from to be able to recruit your perfect co-founders

#47 Choose co-founders you genuinely like

#48 Make sure you (and your co-founders) are all in

#49 Make a simple product, a simple company and think simple thoughts

LIFE QUALITY ENHANCERS

#50 Do what you always wanted to do right now

#51 Notice and appreciate all that went well today

#52 Stick up for your balance

#53 Live life and get a new perspective

#54 Create flow by making shared goals and challenges in your private life

#55 Make a gift or a donation every week

#56 Use your self-discipline to focus on the tasks you are passionate about

#57 Make sure your whole team has the opportunity for balance

#58   Find your sense of self-worth from more sources than just your business

#59   Focus first on your most important friends

#60   Take care of yourself first

STEPS TO TAKE THIS WEEK

#61   Work one hour, and just one hour, at full intensity

#62   Seize the next chance you get for an opportunistic mini-workout

#63   Start tomorrow by doing the thing that has been hanging over your head all week

#64   Spend 2 hours thinking about your purpose in life

#65   Write down what you waste your precious time doing that doesn't significantly add to either your performance or your happiness

#66   Take the day off! Celebrate, digest the *Winning without Losing* message and rejuvenate!

MEET THE AUTHORS:
AN INTERVIEW WITH MARTIN BJERGEGAARD AND JORDAN MILNE

By Roxanne Varza, freelance journalist and
former Editor of TechCrunch France

Martin and Jordan, what brought the two of you together and inspired you to write this book?

Martin: A few years ago, when I first met Jordan, I was thrilled to find a young man from halfway around the planet who shared my passion for this topic. Jordan had just moved to Denmark after working for a VC-funded start-up in London, where he had met numerous entrepreneurs who were at the mercy of their work-dominated lifestyles. Jordan was a natural entrepreneur, but, like me, he didn't want it to control his life.

The more we talked, the more it made sense for us to team up for this project. I, for one, had experienced the horrors of a work-dominated lifestyle when I joined McKinsey at the age of 26. Prior to McKinsey, I had been working on my own ventures in addition to helping my Dad run his company. But when I joined McKinsey I discovered a work atmosphere that was extremely focused on working longer and harder. It was an environment where everyone was fixated on work, which didn't seem advantageous and sustainable to me.

After McKinsey, I wanted to return to a life where I could accomplish everything that I wanted in my professional as well as my private life. I went back to entrepreneurship and over the years, I feel I have discovered how to prioritise things so that my work

doesn't rule my life – and I wanted to share this with other entrepreneurs and future entrepreneurs. I want people to know that becoming a successful entrepreneur doesn't have to mean giving up your life.

Over the past two years Jordan and I wrote this book together. While I was living in Denmark, Jordan was at Cambridge University and in Canada. We met several times in person and also wrote it while we were both travelling the world.

Why does everyone think that being an entrepreneur means making so many sacrifices? Where does this notion come from and how did you discover that it wasn't necessarily the case?

Jordan: I think it's a widely held notion that has been perpetuated for as long as most people can remember. It is simply accepted as a given.

While living in Canada, France, England and Denmark, the common thread amongst most entrepreneurs I met seemed to be that they loved what they were doing, but felt they were sacrificing too much outside work. It was interesting to see that there was so much emphasis put on financial 'winnings' that successful entrepreneurs were actually 'losing' in other ways. Entrepreneurs were bombarded with all the tips in the world on how to be successful, but there were very few role models who stepped forward to demonstrate how to be successful and enjoy the ride at the same time.

I didn't want to accept that the only way to be successful in business was to give up aspects of my personal life. I do want to create the next great company, but I also want to live the balance we are writing about in this book, so I can look back on my life with pride and happiness. No regrets.

I wanted to find people who had succeeded in achieving the best of both worlds. I'm pleased to say that while working on this book with Martin, we did find entrepreneurs who have demonstrated that building industry-changing companies while living a happy and balanced life is indeed possible.

How have you, in your own lives, managed to strike this balance?

Martin: For me the key has been to work with great co-founders.

Before Rainmaking I was mainly doing my ventures as a 'lone wolf' and it translated into too much work with too few results. When you are part of a strong team you can definitely achieve a healthy balance and impressive progress at the same time.

Also, I like to challenge the idea that we are at our most efficient in the office. I know that I have personally come up with some of my best ideas when I have been away from my computer, either running or on holiday. Recognising this has actually helped me to be more efficient and optimise my performance at work.

I also have to give credit to some of my mentors. Being surrounded by successful entrepreneurs who have families and who make time for the things they love outside work has allowed me to apply some of their strategies to my own life.

Jordan: I've definitely found myself engrossed in something and then had to make sacrifices as a result. But I think I am pretty fortunate to have recognised early on that entrepreneurship can be a win–win situation.

For me a big realisation was that happiness leads to success. Not the other way around. Also that health, rest and varied experiences are indispensable to creativity. More working hours doesn't necessarily mean better results.

A big help in the pursuit of success and balance for me has also been learning the strategies of those who have done it.

Find Martin on:
Twitter: @bjergegaard
www.martinbjergegaard.com

MEET THE REST OF OUR ROLE MODELS

Learn more about them at
www.winningwithoutlosing.org

CATERINA FAKE:

Co-founder of Flick'r and
Hunch.com

DAVID COHEN:

Co-founder of TechStars

RANDY KOMISAR:

Partner at Kleiner Perkins Caufield
& Byers

BEN WAY:

Serial entrepreneur and
seed investor

NICK MIKHAILOVSKY:

Founder of Poldo and NTR Lab
(POldo on web searches)

XIANGDONG ZHANG:

Co-founder and President of
3G Portal

TORSTEN HVIDT:

Co-founder of Quartz & Co.

DEREK SIVERS:

Founder of CD Baby

MARKUS MOBERG:

Co-founder of Veritas Prep

CHRISTIAN STADIL:
Serial entrepreneur,
owner of Hummel

PETER MAEGBAEK:
Co-founder of Fullrate

MAXIM SPIRIDONOV:
Serial entrepreneur
and investor

MARTIN THORBORG:
Co-founder of Jubii
and SpamFighter

HENRIK LIND:
Founder of Danske Commodities
and Lind Finans

MORE ABOUT RAINMAKING

Rainmaking has been described as a 'company factory', but what precisely does that mean? The typical reaction we get when introducing people to our concept for the first time is either 'Oh, so you are investing in start-ups,' or 'I get it, you're helping start-ups succeed.' Neither description is completely wrong, but neither is exactly right, and they both miss the point of our core concept. We are not investors, consultants or advisers. We are entrepreneurs, just like any other person trying to build a business from scratch. We come up with ideas, test them on the market, get the first customers, recruit team members, expand, professionalise and grow – and once the business is established, we start all over again.

Where we are different from other entrepreneurs is that we run more businesses simultaneously. Running a whole portfolio of start-ups produces a lot of advantages. Beyond practical things – being able to share resources such as book-keeping and offices, for example – it means that everyone at Rainmaking is constantly experiencing the accelerated learning curve of a start-up.

Today, there are 9 of us who own and actively run Rainmaking. One of us, Morten Bjerregaard Nielsen, is a trained lawyer and the only one of us to work simultaneously across all the companies in our portfolio, helping out with big deals, contracts and legal issues. As for the other 8, each of us focuses on just one company at a time. Unlike us, most investors and advisers won't work full time for years on just one start-up, so that's another big difference between them and us.

After 2–3 years of a project, the team member working on it hands over responsibility to someone else in the team and moves on to found a new venture. When the timing is right, we are always open to exiting each of our start-ups and handing over to other parties to take the project forward in the long term. We don't want to become a conglomerate, and we are not energised by the prospect of thinking about any one company for 20 years. Instead we constantly seek change, opportunities to learn and new adventures – that's what keeps us passionate and enjoying every step of the journey, and what makes Rainmaking a dynamic and exciting place for start-ups.

By 2009 dozens of cool ideas and talented people were flocking to Rainmaking. All these people wanted to work with us, but if we took on too many projects we'd lose what made Rainmaking special. So we decided to launch Startupbootcamp, a 3-month accelerator programme for the best ideas and teams that come our way. As of 2013, Startupbootcamp is active in 6 European cities and works with more than 50 prosperous start-ups every year.

As you may have already sensed, at Rainmaking we are extremely value driven. This is not just a job to us: it's a way of living. The day we founded Rainmaking we formulated and signed a manifesto that still stands. It is based on three Ws: Warm hearted; Whole person; World focused.

Warm hearted: We are all friends, and we want to keep it that way. When going to work in the morning we want the same feeling as when we were kids and went to the after-school club. Approached by someone who wants to join us, the first question on our minds is 'How would I feel if I had to fly to Berlin with this guy?'

World focused: In any kind of profession, it's important to be successful, but it's just as crucial to do it in a way that ends up making you proud. We only launch businesses that are part of the solution in this world, not part of the problem, and elsewhere we have used our entrepreneurial skills to start a school in India, co-found a charity, and host big charity dinners.

Whole person: This is what *Winning without Losing* is all about. We've made Rainmaking somewhere we can pursue our passions without compromising anything else; Rainmaking's central to our lives, but we've built it to fit around them too.

www.rainmaking.co.uk
www.startupbootcamp.org